LIFE IN NUMBERS

LIFE IN NUMBERS

A JOURNEY THROUGH A 9 YEAR NUMEROLOGY CYCLE OF GROWTH AND RENEWAL

LIZZIE FLYNN

Riverside Publishing Solutions

Cover Photo: Courtesy of Sophie Balchin (with thanks).

ISBN (Paperback): 978-1-913012-22-9

The moral right of the author has been asserted.

A full CIP record for this book is available from the British Library.

Published with Riverside Publishing Solutions, Salisbury, UK
www.riversidepublishingsolutions.com

Printed and bound in the UK.

This book is dedicated to my children.

FOREWORD

In 2012 I found myself a single mother of a just turned 2-year-old in the Namibian desert, heading up the 100 plus stunt Makeup Department of the film *Mad Max: Fury Road*, and there began the fury road of what would be the next seven years of my life. Knowing a career as a makeup artist on blockbuster films was no longer going to be in any way conducive with single motherhood, when we finished the shoot I started a business.

A year and a half later I was battling through a divorce, setting up a new home and school for my daughter, and had a business with legs. I needed to find someone to work with me, and along came Lizzie. The job description covered a lot of things, but Personal Development and Numerology were surprise surprise, not in there – luckily for me Lizzie provided them, and it was exactly what I needed.

Lizzie's knowledge and insights helped me to listen to myself and understand how to take my Right Action day to day, month to month, and year to year. She helped me to look inwards, and work out within the framework of numerology, what steps to take next to guide me through a particularly tough time in my life.

Lizzie is a pioneer in her field, and I will always refer back to what I learnt over our period working together. I will always be eternally grateful to her.

Ailie Smith
CEO Creative Media Skills
A Pinewood Studios based Centre of Excellence for Film Training

CONTENTS

Introduction   1

Prologue   Not Everything Starts At The Beginning   4

Year 3   Musings In Malta   9

Year 4   Heartache In Hartlepool   43

Year 5   To The Other Side And Back Again   75

Year 6   No Place Like Home   111

Year 7   Somebody Find Me A Cave   133

Year 8   Money Makes The World Go Round   145

Year 9   Parting Is Such A Sweet Sorrow   173

Year 1   Right Bus – Wrong Way   189

Year 2   Patience Is A Virtue   207

Epilogue   Not Everything Finishes At The End   224

                Personal Year Calculation   226

                Destiny Number Calculation   227

Bibliography   228

Acknowledgements   229

INTRODUCTION

Had I been around in the 6th century BC, when Pythagorus set up his Mystery School, I would have followed him there, keen to delve into the hidden secrets of the Universe. I am a seeker of the truth, and my interest in numerology stems from a long held desire for knowledge about the world, but mostly about myself. Pythagoras was a mystic as well as a mathematician, and he taught that numbers express not only quantity, but quality. He believed that number is the principle and source of all things. It is not only a Universal principle, but also a Divine principle. My modern understanding is, that if we express ourselves according to our numbers i.e. our date of birth and the numbers attributed to our name, then the universe will flow through us, manifesting a truthful and harmonic expression of the Divine.

The first time I came across the meaning of my Life Path Number, the number contained within my date of birth, I felt an enormous resonance with the information I was receiving. This came to me at a time when I was completely lost to myself, and I am grateful for the insights into this ancient source of human understanding which have helped me back on the road to a purposeful existence.

Modern Numerology has developed the Pythagorean idea of number, as a character to be discovered, giving us an easy to understand insight into the symbolic meaning, and esoteric wisdom contained within. The numbers 1–9 each have their own very distinctive quality, and in this book I will be exploring their characters through my personal journey covering a period of nine years. Life is a series of Epicycles running from year 1, the start of the Epicycle, a time of new beginnings and change, through to year 9 which acts as a transition into the next Epicycle, bringing about the tying up of loose ends, completion, and endings. As the tides ebb and flow in tune with the influence of the moon, so do we, in tune with the influence of our numerology. Nine years is a long time, and whilst steering a course in the direction of our dreams and aspirations, we can come across diversions, detours, and delays. But the 9-year cycle shows that there is always a right time to move forward, or to wait patiently, to create or be steadfast, to take action, or to take a back seat.

During my 9-year period of diarising, I would find myself addressing issues including abandonment, stress, self-esteem, anxiety, and anger. My increasing knowledge of the power of this system of self-discovery, helped me greatly in my mental, physical, and emotional wellbeing. This, combined with an introduction to Counselling, Hypnotherapy, Chinese Medicine, Reiki, and other alternative practices, allowed me to unravel past trauma, and deal with issues which had always held me back.

The aim of this book is to guide you on your journey, with the help of my personal experience. It is unlikely that you will pick up the book at the beginning of your current Epicycle, but you can start from where you are, having worked out which Personal Year you are in; or you can simply read from the beginning. I hope that my story will help bring clarity, and understanding, regarding the core meaning and character of the numbers in numerology, which have the same essence wherever they occur. Personal growth is at the heart of the book, and my analysis, starting in a 3 Personal Year, highlights the unmistakable synchronicity of events, leading to my own development during this period. Numerology helped me to look backwards to resolve unanswered questions, look forward to future possibilities, and helped me centre myself in the reality of where I was on my journey.

As you gain greater understanding of the Character of the numbers by diarising, or noting down your experience, you will start to see patterns; cycles within cycles, and enable you to use this information to clarify and develop your own self-knowledge. Draw pictures, write lists, doodle, write poetry, write prose; just write one word. If it resonates with you write it down.

Wishing you an enlightening journey. Lizzie

TO CALCULATE YOUR PERSONAL YEAR PLEASE TURN TO PAGE 224

PROLOGUE: NOT EVERYTHING STARTS AT THE BEGINNING

January 2003, post-divorce, post move, found me at Heathrow Airport on the way to Malta, at the start of what was to be quite a journey. It was only upon later analysis, due to a newly developed interest in all things Numerological, that I discovered I was in the 3rd year of a 9-year cycle, and feeling the overwhelming desire to communicate. It would seem that not all journeys' start at the beginning.

According to Schoolhouse Rock, the American Musical Education series, 3 is a magic number. It is the number of trilogies, trinities, and triangles; and according to modern proponents of the ancient Science of Numerology, it is the number of Communication, and Expression: the number of writers, musicians, artists, actors, dancers, entertainers and creative geniuses. For me it embodies a special magic because it is the Personal Year in which I unexpectedly started writing my diary.

My 9-year period of writing and searching came to me through circumstances, which at the time seemed beyond my control, and I am eternally grateful for the experience; harrowing at times, but full of wonderment, illumination, and growth. Dr Juno Jordan, who is internationally recognised as one of the outstanding numerologists of all time, describes the purpose of each year within the 9-year cycle, through the term Right Action. Lessons learnt in one Epicycle can be taken forward into the next one, and applied with confidence. If the lessons haven't been learnt in the previous Epicycle then they will no doubt return to you for your further edification.

When I started writing my diaries, I did not know of the principle of Right Action. As my experience has expanded, so has my reference to these principles; their esoteric wisdom guiding my thought processes and decision making. However, sometimes even with my newly garnered knowledge, I have pushed back against my internal wisdom and the Right Action principle, and have found myself going way off script, encountering stress, anxiety, abandonment, and self-esteem issues. Luckily, there is always a way to write yourself back into your personal production, and the Right Action principles which you are about to discover, will help you to do this, wherever you are on your journey.

In a world where the image of who we are, and what we stand for is framed in internet technology, there is a danger that we will be taken away from our centre when surrounded by multiple images of other people's realities. It is easy to feel we are not enough.

Computer technology is starting to categorise us as Data Points. Artificial Intelligence is forging ahead, and we stand in the wake of an external avalanche. Adverts pop up from algorithms assigned to who they think we are, what they think we need, and what they think we like, and supermarkets have us taped as a particular type of consumer. But all of these data points have been gathered from our responses to outside influences; in the case of Facebook and Instagram, liking what others have, and how they live. Of course as with everything, used carefully and intelligently, this can shine a light and open your mind to new ideas about what is possible. But beware of the trap. Now more than ever is the time to stand your ground, and build a stage on which to strut your stuff, based on sound personal analysis and a clear understanding about what you value most.

My love of the theatre has prompted me to think of the nine numbers, as characters on a stage, each with its own props and costumes. Each Personal Year acts as a timing device, so that you can channel your efforts towards the Right Action of the year. The Personal Years sit within an Epicycle containing nine years, with the cycle repeating many times in a lifetime.

I have provided a graphic description at the beginning of each chapter/year which gives you the key words associated with the Personal Year in question. The Character Brief is an indication of the overall drive contained within the number, and the costumes and props are just for fun! You may wish to devise your own.

There is an archetypal correlation for each number which can be used as a motif, for example, The Partner, The Builder, The Nurturer, etc. The words contained in the spotlight, are an indication of the energy working at its highest, and most effective level. The words either side of centre indicate when the energy becomes unbalanced.

Self-Mastery happens in the middle.

YEAR 3:

THE COMMUNICATOR

Keywords: Expression · Expansion · Emotion

Underbalanced	Right Action	Overbalanced
critical		*gossipy*
spiteful	ARTISTIC	*quarrelsome*
tactless	CREATIVE	*boastful*
unkind	AMUSING	*patronising*
rude	FRIENDLY	*over-enthusiastic*
unfeeling	POPULAR	*biased*
	ORIGINAL	

FOLLOW THE STRONG DESIRE FOR SELF-IMPROVEMENT

CHARACTER BRIEF
Communicator trying to find their best form of expression

Costume	Props
Waistcoat of Words	Palette of Colours
Coat of Conversations	Party Invitations

■ 33333333333333333333 ■

YEAR 3:

MUSINGS IN MALTA

Your Right Action during your Number 3 Year Personal Year is to believe in yourself and the ideas you have been carrying in your heart and mind, but never expressed. Follow the strong desire for self-improvement. At the end of the year, that which seemed impossible in the beginning should be accomplished.

Dr Juno Jordan
Your Right Action Number

Having cleared check-in, I am left with enough time to purchase a journal; never an easy task when it has to be 'just right'. There is something about the texture, the quality of the paper and the colour, which demands my attention. With the purchase successfully made, the airlines gift of its failure to meet the daily schedule, finds me sitting in front of a cappuccino, writing. I had brought the journal to jot down information on the places I was about to visit, to pass on to a friend. I was also keen to try out my newly acquired drawing skills, gained during a recent trip to Italy, so that I could illustrate my adventure. But the places I was about to visit, were re-visitations of a very personal nature, and not fit for a makeshift guide to the marvels of Malta.

DIARY ENTRY
28th JANUARY, 2003 – HEATHROW AIRPORT

Where is my soul?

This is the question flowing through me, and onto the blank page in my brand new journal, as I sit at one of the world's busiest air terminals. It is as if my pen has been injected with supersonic ink, and I cannot stop writing. I bleed onto the page, keeping perfect meter, poetry moving into prose, and back again through recollections, quiet mindfulness, and optimistic orgasmic outpourings.

The question it seems is a good one, and comes from the overwhelming numbness that I am feeling. It is in desperate need of an answer. I give birth onto the page, releasing the jumbled thoughts which have accumulated in my head on the way to the airport.

BIG STRONG TAXI

Big strong taxi zig-zagging in blatant contradiction towards the terminal, cutting through the traffic with steel like strength into the chaos.

So much control covering pain, denial, rejection, confusion. Answerless living.

What lies beneath waiting to be uncovered – maybe nothing – maybe everything.

So many wishes from so many friends...

How can happiness be so evasive when so many people care?

My heart is rich with wishes, but my soul is bereft.

Life has stolen its core and left a ghost.

Reincarnation needed; rapid restoration required.

How can my life laid bare regain impetus? Can the fight go on? – I am exhausted.

The millennium of 2000 had me feeling alone in the midst of a crowd of friends as we stood staring at the stars. Peeking through the pyrotechnics, I wondered if the millennium bug had changed the world beyond all recognition, and whether I was capable of change on a similar scale. These memories merge with the present, as I stare out at the vast expanse of sky over Heathrow. Silver birds fly in and out at an alarming rate, as I am met with an even earlier image of myself, gazing up at the heavens at the tender age of 12, lying on the grass in the back garden, thinking about the meaning of life. I remember feeling utterly terrified at the awesome possibility of the universe, and complete incomprehension at its vastness. I get the same feeling now if I look for too long; but now I'm not such a scaredy cat, and I can stare it right back in the face. Since then, the meaning of life has been very real to me on many occasions, but those occasions have been fleeting, and outweighed on the other hand, by the complete and utter unknowingness of why we are here.

The year 2000 passed, the bug curled up and went to sleep, and the world carried on. I rolled out of a marriage and into singleness. Two years later, I was standing at the door of major change, after an out-of-the-blue divorce and the move to a new home. My life left like a layer within a palimpsest; rubbed out, overwritten, and incomprehensible.

If you have ever stood on the side of a stage, waiting to make an entrance, you will know the feeling of dread, when you simply cannot remember what on earth your first line is. My problem was that I had never quite learnt my lines properly. Of course I knew everyone else's lines verbatim, but mine... I had for most of my life felt, like I had the wrong script, and I was in the wrong play. I had, it would seem, been ad-libbing my way through life, having created an ill-drawn up character. This not only throws the performer, but also their fellow actors.

As I sat sipping my cappuccino, waiting to be transported to Malta, an island steeped in its own diverse history, I had no idea that I had wandered into a magical 3 year, a year of opportunity, which was to afford me the ability to start to deconstruct the script I had written for myself. As I stare down at the page, I see the words *peace, joy and happiness*, a trinity of treasures. I was ready to grab at anything that was placed in front of me, in the hope that it would lead to one of these states. If only they sold it in bottles at one of the many shops I found myself surrounded by. I'm known to like a shortcut; but there were to be none. Self-improvement was going to take a whole lot of effort.

Many actors, musicians, dancers, artists, and writers vibrate to the number 3 as *'it is they who can interpret and bring forth the silent hidden voices of all things'* *(complete Writings V1 L. Dow Balliott). My voice had become silent during the process of a breakup. Apparently there wasn't anything to say. I had tried to discuss the reasons for the demise of the relationship, but had achieved nothing. I had many questions, but they were met with silence. But I was now in a 3 year and communication it would seem, was an inescapable reality for me. But the conversation I was about to have was with myself, and I was wholly responsible for the answers.

When I look back at my diary, it is abundantly clear that words and communication were at the centre of the year I had entered into, as words flowed out of me with seemingly little effort. Sometimes the words were full of pain, as I tried to express my deepest feelings.

Sometimes there were glimpses of hope, mingling with traces of happiness. They just kept on coming, and I could not stop them. I knew that a dialogue with myself was vital, along with some straight talking, and I hoped that time away would accommodate this. But I found myself with a longing for guidance through the communication of someone else's words. My own voice was deafening me, and I had a metaphorical monkey on my shoulder who would just not shut up. I needed to hear a different perspective on life.

As often happens when you are mulling around an airport bookshop, a book leaps off the shelves, and you just know it has your name written all over it. I am, it would appear to be aided and abetted by a hefty little number entitled, The 5 Stages of the Soul. '*According to many spiritual philosophies our task throughout life, and especially through our middle years is to re-discover the soul locked inside us and return it to its rightful place at the centre of our identity*' (Harry R. Moody & David Carroll). It was as if it had been sitting there waiting for my arrival. The other books on the shelf pale and become invisible. The purchase is made and the journey with my newly acquired travelling companion begins. A glance at the screen shows me that there is still no plane, and so my airport outpouring continues. My newly acquired literary buddy stares up at me, as I pick up my pen and start to address the question of my soul.

DIARY ENTRY
28th JANUARY, 2003 – HEATHROW AIRPORT

I guess I have had many calls from my soul – every time my inner voice shouts, 'is this all there is' a sentence I have heard repeatedly over the past few years, I have known there is more. But if I do not put aside the crap, how can I hope to respond? The call is an overwhelming need to change. Not a minor change, not a change of husband, a change of clothes, change of image, change of location, but a fundamental change. A change back to me; the me I was born with. That person yet to be influenced by parents, siblings, advertising, peers, unrequited love, damaged love, and the contribution of conditioning. But how do you get back there, and when you do get there, then what?

I had left school at 15, knowing that there was something more to me than I could at that stage imagine, but I had disabled myself, with the false belief that my two brothers were more intelligent than me, and that in order to receive love, I had to be like them. I wasn't. I had continued alternating, between trying to be a success in business, and trying to appeal through music, whilst feeling like a fish out of water, and hiding a desire for academic knowledge. I made it to university as a mature student which laid to rest the ghosts of my supposed lack of intelligence, but the 1950's mantra that as I was a girl, I was just going to grow up and get married, was still on a loop in my brain. Indeed I did; three times. But getting rid of the false belief of my lack of intellect, which disappeared the minute the offer letter came through the post from my chosen university, was only part of the story. I stepped away from my course towards the end of my second year, to take up the role of the good wife upon the death of my father-in-law, because I thought that's what I was supposed to do. But I got it wrong, just when it was all going so well. I stepped out of my spotlight, and over a line which wasn't mine to step over.

This action, to all intents and purposes done in the name of love, had left me unfulfilled and unfocused. We move house and I throw myself into a renovation project. Shortly after my husband 'exits stage left' I find myself alone with three children, two cats, a dog, a cockatoo and a baby grand, which I had, at the time of my visit to Malta, just managed to accommodate, in the surreal surroundings of a quirky apartment in an old Victorian country lodge on the outskirts of Ascot.

It was here in January 2003, having lovingly restored the tired interior, when the urge to go away occurred. It was an urge I just could not deny. Malta was chosen quite by chance, having directed the travel agent to find me something not too costly, not too far away, and with a spa. I was exhausted by life, by divorce, by moving, and by setting up a business, and I needed to restore myself.

DIARY ENTRY
29th JANUARY, 2003 – MALTA

Where to look – first stop has to be God – THE God, the ASCOT God, the WESTERN God? But what about the EASTERN God? There are so many. A universal higher being is nearer the mark – there has to be something higher – just look at those stars; but I don't anymore. Too busy rushing around being the someone I have become; an image of myself handed down over the years. The struggle is as old as man. The heroes and heroines of scripture, myth, literature, paintings, and poetry show us the struggle, but the challenges are no longer devils and dragons, but insensitive people, faithless lovers, chronic disease, poverty. The struggle must be the way. Life is a struggle – yes? No? But why must it be? School, work, marriages, failure, children. These things will all still be there, but maybe with the soul's restoration, they will cease to be a struggle, and become a triumph? I must keep looking for the answers.

Having settled into my hotel and with a head full of questions, I hire a car and take myself on an adventure. Malta is an easy island to navigate, and I spend time taking in the sights, drinking coffee, and trying out my watercolour technique. I stumble across the Medieval City of Medina, which is located more or less in the centre of the island, and decide to explore. It is an eerie place and takes me by surprise. It felt as if everyone I encountered there was holding their breath; too scared to speak lest they distort the silence. It is called The Silent City, and it felt as if I was looking in a mirror, staring back at myself saying nothing. When I had stopped for coffee earlier in a nearby town, I had penned my distress at the *'inconsequential treadmill living'* which appeared to be my life. The noise in the cafe in contrast to The Cathedral was deafening. I sat there observing couples tolerating each other, appearing half dead, souls joined together vibrant and alive, and everything in between. There was a dream-like quality about the encounter, and it was as if my soul floated around the cafe, trying to make contact with the human race, so that I could communicate to them my distress. But they were busy, and engaged in their own story. I vowed to work even harder on my restoration, despite the exhausting nature of the process. I had held my breath for long enough. Now was the time to speak up and profess who I was. My silence would get me nowhere.

DIARY ENTRY
29th JANUARY, 2003 – MEDINA, MALTA

SILENT CITY

The Cathedral is dusty, the city is silent – the 'silent city'

God is not here.

How can he be?

It is too cold.

Home, so severely trashed during elevenses with my pen, my words, is sorely missed.

God lives within people's lives, no need for devotion, just love.

I am scared of that love, terrified of the depths of emotion when I allow my soul to move towards the light.

It is love given in a dish... lasagne love.

Layers of compassion, understanding, patience, beauty, unshakable faith.

I think I have been there... why can't I go back?

God must be in Gozo.

He is here in this cafe, but he has vacated The Cathedral.

My words fall directly onto the page, they do not wait to be honed into something resembling Yeats, they just bleed out of me. They ramble and mark the page, making sense, making no sense. They contain more heartache than joy, but as they continue to seep out of me, they begin to clarify my existence and open me up to new ideas. I had spent two solid days and nights downloading my innermost thoughts. Asking questions, answering questions. Making lists, doodling, dreaming, dozing, drinking coffee, drinking wine.

The weather was mostly dark and cloudy, in tandem with my thoughts, stopping me venturing out further. The rain appeared to fall in harmony and empathy with my tears, running down the window pain, obscuring any hope of optimism. But as I progress and download, I feel a lightness starting to return. As always the sun came out again, giving me new impetus.

DIARY ENTRY
31st JANUARY, 2003 – MALTA

CAFE PUCCINI

Sitting in the sun outside the Cafe Puccini, I feel a perfect moment.

When I walked passed earlier, there was a woman in the seat where I am now sitting basking in the sun.

I am now the conqueror of the seat in the sun against the wall.

It doesn't matter that the traffic eight feet away is nonstop;

there is no urgency in their automation.

It is Sunday in Mellieha, and no one is going anywhere except to Church 5.30, 6.00, 6.30, 7.00, 7.30, and 8.00.

It doesn't even matter that my spaghetti bolognese is not made with fresh pasta, as advertised, or that the specks of meat are few and far between.

I am here on my own in the sun.

I am not burdened, like the previous incumbent of the stainless steel throne, by a husband, keen to move on.

Were I here on my own, without the knowledge that there are people in this world that care about me, I would be desolate.

But safe in the knowledge of love I am happy on this windswept island, in the middle of the Med at the end of January.

My writing gives me a form of expression which I have not experienced before, and with each word I write, I start to enunciate my emotions. The same process that occurs through writing, can take place through any artistic endeavour, through music, dancing, sketching, painting, or sculpting allowing the inner voice a way out. When you hit a 3 year, 3 month, 3 day, dance, paint, write, make music, create. Write a plan, write a play, write a list of what you want. Create a list of what you don't want. Doodle, colour in, dip half a potato in paint and slap it on the wall. Make patterns. Make babies.

We are creativity. So many people say, 'I'm not creative', and they can be adamant about this. The word is so often seen in a way that hides its true meaning. When we express ourselves honestly, we are creating. It is such a joyful word that can be used on a daily basis to move us along. It is to do with purpose. Purpose gets us up in the morning, and without purpose there is nothing. Those people in the world who rock the number 3 in a major way, i.e. their Life Path Number, are capable of drawing out the silent voice within us, through their creative endeavour. It might be a song, a drawing, a book, a play, a sculpture. They are able to reflect back to us our inner most emotions, connecting with our soul on a very deep level. My soul has been laid bare many times by a piece of music, or a work of art. I have been stopped dead in my tracks, by plays, novels, and poetry. All of these disciplines have offered me a respite from the storm, and although the experience is sometimes a painful one, I always enter back into the world with a different perspective.

I feel very blessed that I was able to commit my words to the page during my time in Malta. My words had become trapped in my body, and needed to be released. It would seem to me that the numerology of my 3 year, and its connection to Expression and Communication assisted me in this task. Through my writing I found a way to be honest with myself. When we keep things in, they fester, keeping the sun hidden behind the clouds. When your partner asks you if you are OK, and you say, 'I'm fine', when you are not, you harm yourself and you also harm them. You create an illusion. People mostly take you at your word. It is your duty and responsibility to yourself, and to the person asking, to be honest with your communication. With family, with friends, and at work. This of course, can prove incredibly difficult, when faced with the contribution of conditioning whispering in your ears, to 'be polite', to 'just get on with it', to 'act your age', to 'get over it'. A 3 Personal Year is a time to become acutely aware of your words. To take them to task, to become more acquainted with your communication; firstly with yourself, and then with everyone you come into contact with. I used my words in Malta, to express just what it was I wanted in my life, having worked out what I didn't want. I started to dream up new possibilities, using my writing to solidify and expand their potential. I focused on forgiveness as a key to moving forward. This opened a door to optimism, and to a different set of questions, which in turn led to the idea of a different script. Clearly time spent alone is vital to the process, but the 3 year vibration is a very social vibration. It is a year to network, and to get who you are out there. It is a great year to work on the expression of a more truthful character.

Having drawn up a draft of the script I wanted to get onto the stage, I was keen to try out the main character... a new me.

But the hotel is bereft of other guests with which to dally, and I spend many hours sitting in the lobby bar alone, looking across to Gozo. I meditate on the Citadel on the distant horizon, as I continue to search for answers. I am alone except for the barman, who provides my daily caffeine fix, and as the week progresses we become more familiar, giving me an opportunity to come out of the wings and onto the stage.

'ARE YOU WRITING ANYTHING INTERESTING?'

The question floats across the chill air of the lobby and hits me with thundering singularity. I make my way over to the bar and take my place centre stage. I clear my throat and begin to read.

DIARY ENTRY
31st JANUARY, 2003 – MALTA

For the past several hours I have been immersed in the task of recovering my soul. To help me in this task, I have been surrounded by an eerie nothingness, a nothingness crying out to be filled, interrupted only by the occasional request for a cappuccino. My cappuccino is long gone, the effects of the caffeine emerging into the need for another. This marble floored, overdressed, empty hotel, clinging to the top of the rock, which is Malta, is found in the 51st year of my existence. It is unexpectedly a place where a soul can start, with help, to free itself from its many and complicated bindings. The weak winter sunlight coming in through the large salt-stained window, dances on the lobby floor leaving random pattens in its wake. It's official, life is change. This I can rely on.

As I read the barman my words, he responds and unwittingly becomes a vital part of the process of restoration. When a relationship breaks down, there would seem to be an urge to feel desirable, and, despite my lack of holiday haute couture, or in fact any kind of glamour, he is drawn to me and my words. He is clearly bored due to lack of other customers, but even so the attention is fit for purpose, my purpose, the purpose of re-creating myself, and the opportunity arises with a complete stranger to practise my new script.

The offer to show me some of the sights on his day off is taken up. Nervously. But taken up all the same. I drive, he guides, and I am treated to coffee, lunch, and his life story, We talk, we flirt with each other's energy, and pretend we are teenagers joyfully entertaining each other. He was born on the same day as me, albeit it 20 years later, and this happy coincidence does not go unnoticed. Usually when you meet someone with the same star sign as you, things flow. You just seem to 'get' each other. This is a pleasant feeling when they are reflecting back to you all your good bits, the things you love about yourself, but he is also (rather helpfully given my task of self-improvement) also reflecting back to me his scattered energy, and his inability to stick with anything for long. I take note, and I am reminded of all the times that I have fluttered off in another direction, just as I was about to get somewhere. Perhaps this is the source of my unrest, given that I have always been after getting somewhere. We talk and talk and talk because that's what Geminis do.

Silence does not get a look in. Hoorah.

There is a cross hatching between numerology and astrology that I have found cannot be separated. The Gemini energy and the number 5 are joined at the hips, much like Libra and the number 2. I may be in a 3 year, travelling along a path covering 12 months, but my astrology is with me always. I like to think of the number 5 as a hand spread out as far as you can stretch, with all the fingers pointing in different directions. It is a number which is concerned with *freedom and adventure*. I have several 5's in my chart, and this of course leads to lots of adventures, including the one I was having in Malta. However, like every other energy we are given the pleasure of interacting with, there is a need for mastery, and this is an idea that interests me greatly. Jack of all trades and master of none, has been a tag with which I have been acquainted all my life, and although it is in the nature of the Gemini to embrace the many things it is able to do, my interest in numerology seems to have taken me closer to the possibility of self-mastery, having helped me to recognise the truth seeker and analyst in myself. Sometimes things are staring you right in the face, but it is not until you see them written down that they fully resonate. The number 3 energy that I found myself dancing with in Malta, was a good bedfellow for all those 5s. Two odd numbers wanting to communicate with each other in the hope of enlightenment. The nature of the Gemini is to ask questions, and there were many waiting to be answered. I am no good without answers.

My day with the barman feeds my poetic nature and once more enlightenment continues through my pen. Questions are asked, and answered.

DIARY ENTRY
1st FEBRUARY, 2003 – MALTA

LIFE'S LOTTO LINE

My hand taken in his as we cross the road to the Lotto office.

I am his 'lucky charm'.

We stand there with his notion that my numbers are his salvation.

We stand in life's lotto line waiting for a miracle.

For our marriages to be made happy.

For our children to be successful.

For our prayers to be answered.

The line is long, containing as it does the majority of mankind.

I want to traverse my spirituality until the illusions of my life drop away.

I will plant a seed and keep it nourished with the water of hope, contemplation, and struggle until it blooms spontaneously.

I leave my week in Malta having moved forward. I have downloaded, I have felt desired, I have rested, visited the spa, and been massaged, and manicured. I have painted and eaten when and what I wanted. I have been silent, I have been verbal. I have felt pain, I have felt joy. It has been a lifesaver, and I am gratefully restored to a being capable of carrying on with whatever life is about to throw at me next. My diary shows me left with these musings on the nature of communication.

DIARY ENTRY
2nd FEBRUARY, 2003 – MALTA

Sitting in the apple tree at the age of 11, the world was framed in a double focus. In front of me the branch on which I leaned my tender young arms; arms which as yet had not held anyone in a loving embrace, husband, child, lover, friend. In close up the branch was everything I needed it to be: strong, tactile, flexible, interesting, silent. Silent was the problem; it kept me locked in a world where I didn't need to communicate my feelings, and that's where the problems start. As soon as you open your mouth and your being is transported to other people's ears, your words, even honest outpourings, can get lost in translation. If your words are received by some centred, peaceful, beautiful being, who has already managed to work themselves out on the back of an envelope, then you might be in with a chance. Otherwise trouble. Words can become weapons with which to enter into battle, or self-harm especially when you are churning out what you think people are wanting to hear.

The lobby bar becomes my branch, a safe place on which to lean my existence. The barman seduces me with a heady cocktail of laughter, interest, and intent. I can allow myself to be honest, to pour out my innermost secrets; and I do. We lean on the branch together; his soul, my soul, his desires, my dreams, his hopes, my fears, his uncertainty, our longing to explore the mysteries that life holds. The intensity sparks a flame within me, and the cold marble disappears leaving only flesh and blood, flowing in the moment. As we drift towards the end of his shift, my soul once again soars with new life. It is not him. It is not me. It is not us together. It is simply the life force. The unending possibility which life presents if we question, if we search, if we refuse to compromise, if we allow ourselves to be free of the past and stay in the moment.

I return home to my beautiful, but cold and hard to heat flat and carry on with my life. It was only February and there was still a long way to go on my self-improvement quest. The script was in draft form, with a loosely defined character in the lead role. It was a start.

I had a building block on which to stand in the form of a successful business, teaching Musical Theatre to children and adults, and this was growing exponentially. My theatrical partner in crime, whose daughter was in the same class as mine, had the same ideas as me, and as we chatted during an all mothers class lunch, we realised that we were not only on the same page from a creative point of view, but both had the desire to raise some funds for the school. This for me came at just the right time, two years earlier than my trip to Malta in a 1 year; the start of a whole new epicycle and a year of major change.

We were not interested in our daughters being in school productions of classic Musical Theatres shows, where there are six or seven leading parts, leaving the majority backstage waiting for their fleeting moment in the spotlight. We wrote shows specifically to highlight and encourage every child's talent.

I was blessed to have a Libran business partner, who was hot on fairness and great at leadership, and this significantly helped in our endeavour to be inclusive, and to bring out the best in every child and adult. We put on a show at the school after running an after school club for a year, entitled 'Stars in their Eyes'. This gave everyone, including our daughters, an opportunity to shine; to stay in the spotlight for a little longer.

The show was supposed to be a one off, but given the success of the enterprise we managed to persuade the Head Teacher, to let us carry on with the after school Musical Theatre Classes. My time building the Musical Theatre Company aptly named FASBAT (Find A Space and Be A Tree) ran alongside my post-divorce personal development, and covered a whole epicycle. Our initial marketing image was a rather cheeky looking acorn running off to plant itself. I didn't realise it at the time but that was exactly what I was after, a replanting of my potential.

The FASBAT partnership was officially formed in 2002; the year before I started writing my diaries. Synchronistically the number 2 is all about **Partnership** and **Co-operation**, and is linked the Astrological sign of Libra. For me, this blessing came at just the right time and acted as a strong foundation. As the company grew so did the FASBAT family. My partner and I both loved the theatre, and had been involved in its magic from an early age. Me through an Amateur Dramatic company in Slough, and my partner through a Dance School in Shanklin on the Isle of Wight. She had turned professional, leaving the island for the bright lights of the mainland and beyond. We came together by chance, as so often happens in life, at what appeared to be just the right time for both of us. We were keen to pass on our love of all things theatrical, and FASBAT was the perfect vehicle.

It takes a lot to stand on a stage and perform, and it's not for everyone. But we are performing on our own personal stage, wherever we place ourselves, and it's our responsibility to show the world who we really are. Even when we think we are invisible and just standing around in the wings, our energy is transmitted out into the ether and into the energy field of whoever we are standing next to. Showing the world the business of who I was, was clearly at the forefront of my mind during this time, and confidence in myself was key.

I loved to watch how our pupils became more self-assured during the rehearsals, and I took even more pleasure watching them shine in their own particular way during the performance.

Stepping into the spotlight had an effect on even the most nervous performer. Observing the joy on their faces and the faces of the audience never failed to warm my heart and lift my spirit. The Head Teacher was later to refer to 'the individual triumphs' to be seen in every child; some were small, some were monumental, with each child learning to stand in their own space projecting themselves into the world.

We started each session with everyone standing up and stating their name. Shoulders back, head up; my name is... This proved very hard for some people to do, adults as well as children. I remember one child found this experience particularly difficult. She had withdrawn into herself and wouldn't speak her name. After three terms she eventually found the courage to stand on the stage and say her name. The joy experienced by everyone in the room was immense, and her confidence grew exponentially from that moment on.

Our birth name is fundamental to our existence, and according to numerology holds a very special set of vibrations. In her book *The Romance in Your Name*, Dr Juno Jordan states that *'the name you were given at birth tells the story of your destiny.*

All other names, nicknames, changes of name, or married names, are but channels through which your destiny is worked out and expressed. At first you may not be 100 per cent in performance, but if you keep on trying you will find it easy and finally gain the love, success, and repeated rewards it has promised you.' It is a book I highly recommend.

When you meet someone for the first time, you can tell if they are comfortable in their own skin by the way they introduce themselves. It is a mini performance. People so often withdraw from their centre, and this is visibly noticeable when they say their name.

Saying something in your head is one thing, speaking it out loud is another. It can be a very uncomfortable experience, but it gets easier as you find your strength and confidence through truthful self-expression. The more you speak your truth, the more you become your truth. Visualising yourself on a stage speaking confidently to a receptive audience, is a technique I have engaged with many times. During the following nine years I would at times find myself with a very shaky voice, and an overwhelming desire to be understood as I re-wrote my script. The phrase 'speak your truth, even if your voice is shaking', is now embedded into my psyche, reminding me to stick with who I am, although the urge to wander off into the wings and hide behind the curtain can sometimes trip me up.

The titles of the shows created at FASBAT during my nine years of diary writing, show a startling synchronicity between what was going on in my life, and head, and what was expressed onto the stage. As I moved through the Epicycle I was exploring themes such as Self Expression, Foundations, Confidence, Service and Love and the titles, which were to include 'We Can Do It', 'The Dating Game', 'What Is It About Love', and 'The Greatest Show On Earth', included elements of the challenges

I was working through. These were of course hidden behind the singing, dancing, and greasepaint, but embedded into the script. They were in tune with the essence of each Personal Year I was traversing, and although I could not see this at the time, with analysis it is startlingly obvious.

This highlights to me the role of the subconscious in the every day. We still know very little of the work that goes on behind the scenes, in our subconscious as we make our way through life. The things that represent our conscious awareness, are simply 'the tip of the iceberg'. The rest of the information that is outside of conscious awareness lies hidden below the surface. Although we may be unable to discern this information, it still exerts an enormous influence over our behaviour.

This ties in with the unconscious influence of number vibration and its esoteric meaning on a daily, monthly, yearly basis. Speaking our truth under the vibrational influence of the number 3, supports our ever present need to be understood, whether this be on a 3 day or during a 3 month or 3 year. The negative side of the 3 energy is that words can be used to destroy as easily as they can be used to create. They can generate havoc instead of positivity and joy. Words can rush out of your mouth causing great harm. Finding a way to speak your truth without harming others is a key feature of a 3 Personal Year, and this needs close attention when the 3 is in operation.

MAY, 2003

Having been able to churn out a few words at the beginning of the year, I now feel I have a book in me! I buy the 'Art of Writing' to help me in this task, and turn to the chapter on Creating Characters. The exercise is fun, and suggests that you place yourself somewhere where you can observe the human race. You then start to fill in a profile, through observation of some poor unsuspecting person, who is trying to go about their business in privacy. I am drawn to this as there is an opportunity to drink more coffee, be on my own, and indulge myself in some scribbling. I take myself to my local cafe, and place myself in the corner and wait... it doesn't take long before my victims start to arrive.

DIARY ENTRY
SUNDAY 11th MAY, 2003 – SUNNINGHILL

Kevin was a sweet man. He cared deeply about his job, his family, and his friends. He worked hard as a surveyor, albeit mundane and routine after all these years. It sometimes took people quite a while to transcend Kevin's outward appearance. His curly hair, shiny shoes, and neatly pressed shirt hid the inner Kevin. His childhood had been very ordinary, culminating in the 2.1 obtained at one of the 'red brick' universities. Marriage followed rapidly, along with the 2.4 children whom he adored. The early years which carry us through to middle age, had for Kevin gone smoothly, as smooth as his freshly pressed shirt...

I bore of Kevin, and move onto the next person.

The all-American boy, now well into middle age sits propped in the corner. The crew cut, an attempt to defy the signs of balding, blended with the tan, making the gold Rolex stand out like a beacon against the faded decor of this once popular bar. The new trendy 'life-style' bar/cafes with internet access, which had recently sprung up in the neighbourhood, had left this once vibrant hub far behind in the popularity stakes. The clientele had been seduced by the bright stainless steel...

A woman catches my eye and I turn over onto a clean page.

She sat with her long blonde hair flowing down her back, sipping her latte, and nibbling at her croissant. The daily paper, a tabloid of some sort, flicked through. Her jeans and designer top were snug around her fit body, belying the years of comfort eating prompted by unhappiness and pain. The trendy sunglasses cut down the glare from the sun, as it streamed through the large windows out onto the world. She wore an enormous diamond ring on her wedding finger; symbolic perhaps of the dazzlingly hopeful start to her now faded relationship. She hadn't married her third husband thinking he would be one in a long line; she had married him thinking he would be the last. She was, underneath all of her outer appearance, a kind and caring person, who always tried to encourage people. She loved to make a difference in people's lives, but lately she had lost her spark, lost her centre, and lost her purpose. She had been born in an era when women stayed in the kitchen, and men brought home the bread. She seemed to have fallen through a transition gap. She looked at women who had made it in the business world, had successful marriages, and seemed to be making a difference. She stood astride the past and the present in so many ways.

She wanted a new start. She wanted to express herself fully and joyfully, but what she didn't want, was to walk away from this marriage. She had run from her first two marriages, trying to find her true identity, trying to work out what really did matter to her, and what constituted the good life. She had vowed never again to be unfaithful, even when challenged by unhappiness. She had stuck to this and it was a source of pride. But sitting here just 'flicking' through the pages of life, she had started to realise, that in order to go forward, she had to go backwards to sort out all of the unresolved matters, which kept her away from confidence, success, and happiness...

As I sat there sipping my coffee, I wondered if maybe, I could start myself again on a new page? But there was so much to rub out before I could start to re-model. I abandon the exercise and head for home with much food for thought.

My writings in Malta see me musing that 'one week in Malta does not equal peace. It is just a beginning along a winding road', a road which I willingly step onto again, when some dear friends invite me on a trip to Medjugorje in the heart of Bosnia. Medjugorje is a town located in the Herzegovina region of Bosnia and Herzegovina, around 25 km southwest of Mostar, and close to the border of Croatia. Since 1981, it had become a popular site of Catholic pilgrimage due to Our Lady of Medjugorje and an alleged series of apparitions of the Virgin Mary to six local children.

This feels very much out of my comfort zone, and budget, but my very generous friends, who can see my current loss of direction, very kindly fund the trip, enticing me with the prospect of a night in a 5 star hotel in the city of Dubrovnik.

I feel very blessed to be travelling again so soon after the last trip, and take to the road in the company of some very special people. I relish the opportunity to continue writing, and being a singleton, I am very pleased to be able to hide behind my pen and notebook. Once again my journal becomes a place of retreat, reflection, creativity, and growth.

DIARY ENTRY
JUNE, 2003 – BOSNIA

Dubrovnik sparkles in the sunlight. The golden rays shine down upon a city, restored to its former glory, after the mindless devastation inflicted by war. The manicured beaches and recently restored stonework blend effortlessly into the medieval splendour which anchors the city to the Adriatic. The sea, which has remained constant, reflects the glory and hope evidenced by the people of Croatia. I am here, a guest on my way to Medjugorje, a holy place in the heart of Bosnia to work on some restoration of my own. I had met the Parish Priest at a dinner party, and he appeared to be one of the good guys. So with the promise of lots of sun and cocktail hour, I set out somewhat apprehensively on my journey. I am a Protestant, they are Catholic. I hope they are feeling ecumenical.

Before we leave the city, we lunch in the shadow of the cloisters. The smell of garlic mingles with the oleander, heightened by the heat of the day. I tentatively attempt to infiltrate the communion which exists between the group. The care and love which they quietly lavish on each other washes over me, draws me in, and gives me a window into the joy they feel in each other's company. We attend mass at the Church of St Blaise, and I am struck by the beauty of our surroundings. The Church is small, and holds you firmly between its gloriously bedecked walls. My eyes are drawn to the crucifix to the left of centre aisle. I am humbled by the sorrow tenderly portrayed through the exquisite carving. A Scotsman, a Canadian, and an Englishman join together at the altar to minister to us.

They haven't met before, but come together in perfect harmony through the Eucharist. I am struck by the leader of our party, who kneels in prayer on the cold stone floor. She is an extremely elegant woman who radiates a very special warmth. I look forward to spending more time in her company. In fact, I unexpectedly look forward to the company of every single person in the group. We have been together for such a short time, but already strong bonds are beginning to form.

Our spiritual leader Father Richard, dressed in priestly black, complete with designer shoes, is a rather fetching mixture of English gentleman, Richard Chamberlain, and boyish charm. His voice is resonant and gentle, and when used to deliver the rosary, traces of Latin which still link the liturgy of the church, has the ability to transport you back to the Middle Ages when the voice of Catholicism rang out from every tower.

As we approach our destination at the start of our Pilgrimage, he suggests we do 'The Rosary'. I wonder as I gaze at the sheep dotted around the hillside, just what this entails. Rosary beads of every description are pulled from the hand luggage, in anticipation of the ritual. The origins of the Rosary are traceable to the 12th century when using a string of beads, meant the uneducated and illiterate faithful were able to have a closer participation in the liturgy of the Church. The words of the Rosary are repeated time after time, and seem unnecessary repetitions, but the meditative effect of this ritual soon infiltrates my whole being. My mind wanders back to nights spent counting relatives of the outdoor population, by which we are currently surrounded, and I wonder whether a round of the Rosary would work just as well when sleep becomes evasive.

As we enter Medjugorje, I see we are in a valley surrounded by hills. We pull up outside our hotel, the Lucia Maria, which is approached down a dusty track. From the outside it looks like the results of bad planning regulations, with a design enhanced by watching too many Westerns. The welcome however, is as warm as the outside temperature. Our Leader organises our keys, and we are packed off to our very basic, but clean rooms to freshen up. It is in stark contrast to our 5 star beginnings in Dubrovnik, the bait used to get me there, and I wonder how my spoilt little 5 star self will adjust.

In the morning, after a simple breakfast of bread and jam, we make our way to Mass, in the Church which lies at the centre of this tiny village. The building seats at least 600 and seems disproportionate to the needs of the village, considering it was built 22 years before the 'apparitions' started. It stands as a reminder to the un-converted, perhaps that God moves in mysterious ways.

The pale yellow exterior of the church blends gently into the surrounding hillsides, as its twin towers stretch up towards the pale blue sky, which provide a beautiful background, for the plain black crosses which sit atop their pinnacles. The interior of the Church is architectural simplicity. Modern stained glass panels, placed high above the body of the church, do not distract from the clean space. Mass is celebrated throughout the day in many different languages. You could be forgiven for thinking briefly that you are in Disneyland, as crowds of people stream through one door and out of another, ready for the next show. But as silence descends, the outside world is swept away, and peace is restored. A posse of Priests collect at the altar. The international diversity is unclear until they come forward to share in the liturgy. The mass for the most part is in English, with a smattering of Latin.

The different dialects sing out creating an entrancing harmony. I hear a conversation from the pew behind me, bemoaning the loss of the exclusively Latin Mass over the past 40 years. 'Once I was able to celebrate mass anywhere in the world', says the complainant;

'now it is difficult to follow'. Despite the obvious advantages to the 'less educated and illiterate faithful', I have to admit he has a point. My mind wanders back to the signs for 'Big Mac', just a stone's throw from the Church, and think of the people on the planet worshipping at a very different alter as they queue, not for the sacrament of the Church, but the delights of the fast food revolution.

After lunch, we wander across the fields and sit under the trees on white plastic chairs. The trees give little relief from the soaring heat of the afternoon sun. There is a large gathering, and we are present to hear Sister Emmanuel. We sit under the gaze of a beautiful white statue of the Virgin Mary. As the crowd quietens, the noise of the cicadas rises to a crescendo, and we collectively lean forward in anticipation of straining our ears, to listen to the diminutive figure dressed in white. But we needn't strain. Our fears are blown away on the gentle breeze, as her message is clearly and beautifully communicated. No amplification necessary. She knows what she wants to say, and it is delivered and expressed with confidence clarity and conviction. I ponder upon what it is that I want to say, how I want to say it, and by what means I will use to deliver it. Once again, my pen has taken to paper, and I wonder whether my voice could be heard through writing.

When we return to our hotel for lunch, we are about to be made homeless due to a double booking. Fifty-five Italians are arriving the next morning, and there is apparently no room at the inn. This has been an ongoing saga, and cause for concern throughout the trip. We have constantly felt the threat of displacement, due to the chaos of so many souls trying to congregate in one place.

Compassion is needed, forgiveness for mistakes is required. Some people have mastered this. Others clearly not. I am grumpy and sit firmly within the 'clearly not' category, the number 3 energy fuelling my ability to be critical.

The heat here is having an effect on me which I have never experienced before. It's as if it is melting away my ability to keep my deepest emotions hidden. Each day I feel weaker, and on the verge of a breakdown. This is strange, as I also feel the most peaceful I have ever felt in my life. There are many hundreds of people in this place, but the silence is deafening. I am struck by the rows of confessionals which line the streets of the main area. Like portable toilets, a place to ditch the unwanted in you. I am not a Catholic, I am no longer 'religious', but I am struck by an overwhelming desire to have my confession heard. This is tricky. If I ask Father Richard to hear my confession, I know that I am putting him in a compromising situation. The rules are: you have to be Catholic. But I am in search of my soul, so I can't let hundreds of years of convention stand in my way. I will have to trust in human kindness. Surely that is the central message. I take the risk. I ask. The request is taken away overnight, and granted the very next day. I sit in the soaring heat on a ramshackle porch, surrounded by the sounds of the day and the red dusty soil, and pour out years and years of pent up heartache. The silence disappears.

It is painful. It is noisy.

I am truthful.

I am uncomfortable, and I am quite unexpectedly absolved.

In my 9 month, in my 3 year, I find closure on a multitude of past misdemeanours, mistakes and misguided actions. My voice has shaken with the utterance of each and every word, and I am exhausted. But the feeling of release brings immediate emotional improvement. I sleep for the rest of the day and awake refreshed.

AS WE TRAVERSE A PERSONAL YEAR, WE TRAVEL THROUGH A DIFFERENT VIBRATIONAL EMPHASIS EACH MONTH. AS ALWAYS, THE GENERAL THEME OF EACH NUMBER REMAINS THE SAME. THE RIGHT ACTION OF THE YEAR CAN BE ENHANCED, BY LOOKING CLOSELY AT THE MONTHLY VARIATIONS. WHEN YOU ADD THE CALENDAR MONTH NUMBER TO YOUR PERSONAL YEAR NUMBER YOU ARRIVE AT THE PERSONAL MONTH NUMBER,
i.e. PERSONAL YEAR (3) + JUNE (6) = PERSONAL MONTH (9).

The next day I climb to the top of the mountain along with many other pilgrims. I wonder as I walk, what they are looking for. Are they looking for the same thing as me, or something completely different? I observe a married couple from the group, and am envious of their joint devotion, to each other, and to their belief system. I am walking with Lady Villiers, who has Catholic devotional grit in every step she takes. She is in her 80s, and nothing is going to stop her reaching the top. She may be a Lady, but she was in the Belgium Resistance and escaped to England via a treacherous journey across the Pyrenees. The Chinese philosopher Lao-tzu (604 BC–531 BC) said that 'A journey of a thousand miles starts with just one step', and I recall this as I continue upwards, one foot in front of the other. When I reach the top, I am blown away by the amount of people who congregate at the foot of the enormous cross.

From somewhere comes the urge to sing the Lord's Prayer. The version, which is whizzing around my head, is the version penned by David Fanshawe, the self-styled Ethnomusicologist who met my first husband whilst travelling through Africa. He had taken a small stereo tape recorder on his journey, and would persuade local musicians to play for him. Returning to the United Kingdom in 1972, with several hundreds of hours of recordings made during his travels, Fanshawe used the material to compose what became his best known work, African Sanctus, which includes a very beautiful version the Lord's Prayer. At dinner one evening he said, 'Before they nail down the lid of my coffin, I want to have made a difference in the world'. This has stayed with me always, and as I stood at the top of the mountain, singing this version of a prayer I have known since I was a small child, I am aware that I have an opportunity to rebuild – to create the life I want to live, to make a difference before I cast off my mortal coil. As I rest at the top of a mountain, I imagine myself sitting on a box full of all the good things about my life, my talents, my passions, and my internal wisdom flowing out of the box, and down the mountain, being of service to the world. The word forgiveness is etched on my heart.

Numerology can seem very confusing at first, but once you are au-fait with the general themes, you will start to dance with their individual energies, and observe the synchronicity and timing of life's journey. When we are at the centre of the energy of each individual number, we are working at our highest level, expressing ourselves confidently and truthfully. It is easy to see what happens to that energy, when fear steps in and we step out of the spotlight.

My return from Bosnia leaves me feeling exhausted but optimistic. I had started the year with a desire for self-improvement, and I felt as if I was now in a much better place to move forward, with renewed purpose.

YEAR 4:

THE BUILDER

Keywords: Practical · Stable · Organised · Determined

Underbalanced	**Right Action**	**Overbalanced**
impractical		*rigid*
lazy		*stubborn*
uncertain	PATIENT	*headstrong*
unadaptable	CAREFUL	*insensitive*
inefficient	RELIABLE	*slow*
tired	PRACTICAL	*narrow-minded*
	ORGANISED	
	CONSISTENT	
	DEPENDABLE	

FIRM FOUNDATIONS WILL WIN THE DAY

CHARACTER BRIEF
Cornerstone of society, loves to lay down solid foundations

Costume	Props
Shoes of Stability	Bucket of Building Blocks
Pashmina of Patience	Tin of Endurance
Limitation Leggings	Large List

■ 444444444(22)444444444 ■

YEAR 4:

HEARTACHE IN HARTLEPOOL

This can be a year to manage things, especially your health. It's a time to set things in order, set up systems and lay down solid foundations for your future. Getting a home, getting married, having a family, getting insurance – all of these are the foundation pieces for our life. Needless to say, a 4 year takes a lot of hard work.

Another facet of the 4 Personal Year that you may be working on, is going back into the roots of the family dynamic, in order to sort out your relationship to the early childhood drama. This work is usually called 'family of origin' work, and (so fitting for the 4) it's about getting to the root of the problem. For this reason, this year may feel like the year from hell; it's very hard to dig deep, and reset the foundation pieces of your adult life.

Kay Lagerquist and Lisa Lenard
The Complete Idiot's Guide to Numerology

I love drawing squares. I like to add windows (with curtains), a door, a roof, a chimney (with smoke), and to finish it all off, a lovely path with a picket fence. It makes me smile. Sometimes I add mountains covered in trees; sometimes there is a pond, complete with ducks. The sun is shining high in the sky, and the birds are happily flying around to their heart's content.

What does yours look like I wonder?

There is no obvious emotion attached to anything when I draw the image, which is my go-to doodle when sitting in tedious committee meetings, or used as avoidance when trying to write. It often shows up on the page without me noticing. Always the same square house, with just a few variations. Every number has a geometric shape, a colour association, and also a musical note. The colours for the number 4 are green and blue, the musical note is an F and the geometric shape a solid reassuring square. Another wonderful use of squares, if you can manage to wrestle the Duplo from a nearby child, is to build a tower. You can build a whole street of dwellings from single lines of square bricks. A New York skyline is a favourite of mine, and although on mass they will look strong stood next to each other, let the aforesaid mentioned child near them and they will topple over extremely easily. However, build a solid square block, and fill it in with solid square blocks, and it will become virtually indestructible. It is the blocks inside which gives it strength.

The number 4 appears in many of the systems by which we establish our place physically. There are four cardinal points to the compass, four seasons, four elements: fire, water, earth, and air, and the liberal arts of geometry, astronomy, music, and arithmetic are all important in understanding the other sciences. The four-sided symbol which makes up my favourite doodle, was considered sacred by the Pythagoreans because it represented the beginning of form.

If we look at our life in terms of blocks we can see that they can give us a great sense of security. However, they also have the power to entrap. Parental blocks, sibling blocks, learning blocks, play blocks, security blocks, friendship blocks, work blocks, etc. Just like Lego blocks we have the power to add them, and take them away, or indeed put the ones we don't want in a box and hide them away under the bed. Have you ever tipped the lego box onto the floor and then been overwhelmed by the task of sorting out the individual blocks in order to start to build something new? If you stick with it, the pleasure at the end of the task is immense, but sometimes the temptation just to shove it all back into the box and leave it until another day wins. In a 4 Personal Year, patient perseverance is key.

During my 3 Personal Year, I had sat on the roof of my world, gazing at the stars, and dreaming up possibilities. Every time I had an idea, I would write it down and pop it in an imaginary box. I wanted to use these ideas to shore up my foundations. But there was a phantasmagorical elephant in the box taking up all the space. The only way to deal with it, was to dismember it bit by bit and dispose of it. Gruesome, difficult, hard work. A key message of the 4 year, is there are no shortcuts; stability is achieved through order and process. Not only did it require me to dispose of the elephant, but I was soon to realise that I had to first take down the house brick by brick, so that I could completely rebuild my foundations, rather than just shore them up.

Leaving my 3 Personal Year, a year of such discovery and adventure, and one that suits my overall plethora of odd numbers, was a challenge for me. I have a feeling that it always will be. The number 4 is linked to Taurus, the astrological sign before mine. It is an Earth sign. I am an Air sign. At its best it is patient, careful, reliable, practical, organised, consistent, and dependable; all the things you need to build something solid during the 4 vibration. I can of course be all of these things at various times. We all can when minded too, but the slow, and sometimes stubborn energy, often clashes with my fast moving mercurial temperament, which wants to explore, talk, communicate. The 4 energy wants to pin me to the ground, and keep me focused.

My very grounded Taurean daughter, has been heard to say when I am in full flow, flying around my head, looking at everything from every perspective possible, 'Why don't you stop talking, and just do it'. In astrological terms it is said that you should always draw on the sign before yours, as it has a lot to teach you. I have to agree that the idea is a sound one, and my mercurial Gemini nature is grateful for the lesson. The basic principle applies to the Taurean energy, which can become stuck, dull, and over cautious if it's not careful. For a Taurus drawing on the fiery Aries energy, the sign before itself, can be of great benefit, as it can be used to stoke the fire, and get the starting energy moving again. Sometimes the Gemini needs to slow down and ground itself. Sometimes the Taurus energy needs to fire up. It is the same for every astrological sign. We can't always be centre stage, firing on all cylinders and sometimes standing in the wings observing other performers, can be of great benefit.

The number 4 is without doubt, the number which has given me the most trouble in my life. Sounds a bit silly doesn't it, to say a number could be so disruptive, but believe me it can. The number 4 is missing in my Total Expression Chart, which is the chart derived from the name given at birth, and annotated in full on my birth certificate. Missing numbers are referred to as Karmic Lessons in numerology and any missing numbers in your chart, offer great potential for growth.

Some people have several numbers missing in their chart. However, just one is enough to cause havoc to a Gemini with a preponderance of 5s. So the lesson of the 4, is a lesson of patience and steadfast endeavour, without short cuts; a good way to build solid foundations. Right, got it. Unfortunately 'short cuts', as my needlework teacher Miss Brocklebank remarked, was my middle name. I remember making my first garment in her class at secondary school. 'So let me get this straight, you have to put pins all the way around the pattern, you have to tack the darts, and you have to do everything in order, as per the instructions'. No way. I can do it much quicker than that. I can just cut around the pattern using a few pins, forget the tacking, and just guess what goes next. Ta da, my very first garment – seer sucker culottes – not exactly the easiest choice on the planet. Poor Miss Brocklebank was torn between admonishing me for not following the order, and praising me for being bold. My seven 5s make me bold, adventurous and also a risk taker; someone who can jump from one thing to another, and do several things at the same time. I love change, and without change I am nothing. I just find it so damn hard to sit and do anything for any length of time. When there is something I need to do, which requires staying in one place and focussing for any length of time, I feel the need for change, and I am known to move my furniture around by way of avoidance. Easier to move furniture than stay on task. But I have finally learnt that I will achieve nothing using this avoidance technique apart from a bad back! I have also learnt that the need to run away from the task comes from fear, and lack of confidence.

The foundations laid in my early life, had always been shaky, and had haunted me for years causing all sorts of problems, running away before rejection being one, and the fear of abandonment the other. As I stood on the edge of my 4 Personal Year, I had no idea that I would be taken down a path, that would lead me back to my deepest feelings around my perception of family and home. It would take me in through the door of my perfect looking house, and lock it behind me until I had overcome obstacles, patiently picked through some very uncomfortable memories, and dealt with the seemingly immovable and imaginary elephant. My life to date had left me with three broken marriages, a suitcase full of disempowering beliefs, an unfinished university degree and three displaced children. But I had hit a 4 year in my 5th Epicycle, and the time had come to rebuild. No running. No shortcuts. No abandonment.

If your foundations are not built on honesty, they will crumble. They will hold for a while, and do a passing impression of stability and longevity, but in the end the cracks will start to show. There are so many things I had not been honest about, with myself, and with others. So far, not so good then. Just an actor playing a part. I did not think for a second that the aftershocks of the earthquake I was about to encounter, would be so fundamentally significant in my progress, but once the home and family rubble is on the floor, the order somehow needs to be restored, and the number 4 is the baby to help you do it.

Put a sponge in a bath, and it will soak up the water until it becomes waterlogged. As children we absorb everything, ideas, words, and images, which come at us from every direction. Home, school, friends, media. Our foundations are built on these early experiences, and although it is entirely possible to move forward from childhood to adulthood, presenting something which looks like a successful life, if our beliefs and ideas don't match our inner wisdom, we are destabilised. Teaching children to communicate and talk about their feelings, and listening carefully to what they are saying, has got to be one of the foremost responsibilities of a parent. Easily said, and hindsight is a wonderful thing. I can recall rushing around like a headless chicken, trying to get everything done instead of stopping to listen properly to mine. We have become waterlogged with the requirements of modern living, leaving society with some very difficult avenues to navigate. We are surrounded by the noise, which has enveloped the 21st century and drawing on the 4 energy to slow things down, is a useful tool for anyone.

The lockdown crises of 2020, a year when the whole world effectively shut down, shows the power of the Universal Year Number. Clearly an unprecedented example. The Universal Year is a standalone number, and is the number used to derive your Personal Year (refer to page 224). As I write this the airwaves are full of the rhetoric of the 're-build', the slow journeying back to a 'new normal'. I am blown away by the synchronicity of the numerology of our current time in history and the numerology of our leaders who are talking in terms of cross party co-operation. 2 is the number of co-operation, partnership, consideration and understanding. Boris Johnson after a feisty 'Get Brexit Done' 1 Personal Year in 2019, now sits firmly in the middle of a 2 Personal Year in 2020. The new leader of the Labour Party was born on the 2nd September and also has a 2 Life Path Number. Seriously, I couldn't make it up!

The 4 is the number of obstacles, dead ends, difficulties, limitation, hard work and endurance; there is a long way to go, but my hope through all of this is that foundations are strengthened, co-operation becomes exemplified, and that when we reach 2021 – a Universal 5 year there will be movement, progress and change for the good of all mankind.

I thought that the ideas I had dreamt up during my 3 year, would somehow just materialise, but that's not the way it works, at least not in my experience. I had made no resolutions. I didn't really have a masterplan, I just had the desire to grow, move forward, and somehow succeed in a way that I had never done before. I work very quickly. I can multitask, flit from one thing to another, and generally make things happen before patience can even be given breath. But this time that wasn't going to work. There is a need to be specific when dreaming things up, otherwise the Universe, and more importantly our neural pathways get confused. Unless we re-build these pathways, we trundle along the same old ones on automatic pilot, repeating our mistakes. Now it was time to fly the plane myself and change the route.

I didn't possess many certificates with which to fly my plane. My first, a certificate for cooking an omelette, my one and only school prize, was frankly as much use as a blunt pencil, despite the fact that it remains in my 'important things' box under the bed. I managed between the age of 38–41, somehow to crawl my way through to Grade 5 piano and Grade 3 cello. As a child I had taught myself to play hymn tunes in the garden shed where the piano had been discarded to make way for the radiogram. I loved it out there in my musical cave. Unfortunately I was using all the wrong fingers; they were recognisable as hymn tunes, but the foundations I had built them on, would not stand the test of even a snippet of Mozart, let alone a whole movement.

That had to be undone in order to progress, and to perform scales to a scary examiner with an eagle eye. Scales and arpeggios are the foundation of musical accomplishment, and learning to play a musical instrument, is a wonderful example of the practical and organised nature of the number 4. In order to play well you have to build things slowly; process is required. I of course, with my propensity for shortcuts, will always try to play a piece straight through, leaving out most of the notes in the process. I can get the gist of the piece, but that is about all. There is no mastery, no finesse. The tune is there, but the true nature of the piece isn't. Gillian Oakes my rather wonderful piano teacher wasn't having any of that! In between our howls of laughter, which took up most of the lesson, she managed to coach me to the finish line, and I am eternally grateful. It is better to consistently practice for five minutes every day, one bar at a time, until you are able to start to build, adding the bars together, rather like building blocks. This brings stability and confidence, which is generally followed by progress, slow but sure. I had previously experienced the terror of putting myself in for my Grade 3 cello exam, without the blessing of my teacher, and against his better judgement. My head and fingers had obviously gone off at a tangent, rather like my life, and I passed by the skin of my teeth. I froze when asked to do a particular scale, that I just didn't know well enough due to lack of consistence and diligent practise, and it taught me a sound lesson; the lesson of the 4. No short cuts. I passed the exam, apparently due to the feeling I had for the piece, but the foundations felt very shaky, and I knew they would not stand the test of time. But if scales really aren't your thing, just play, play, play. The ceiling won't collapse. I just needed some certificates in my life, other than the one I had for making omelettes!

I arrive in March of my 4 Personal Year, which equates to a 7 month, a month where study and contemplation are key themes, along with an invitation to attend a personal development event at the Excel Centre in London. The invitation came from a dear friend who has persuaded me to go with her. She is open to all things spiritual, exciting, and fast moving, and is an exquisite bundle of love. However she is not without her own demons, and we decide to take our demons for an outing. The number 7 is a seeker of wisdom, and is concerned amongst other things, with the accumulation of knowledge, internal knowledge of a spiritual nature. It is an odd number (in more ways than one), and therefore the opportunity should be taken for reflection, and a review of your inner self whenever it occurs. You know those days when you just want to ponder, or be on your own, withdraw? Well you are probably under the influence of the 7 energy. So take time out to be quiet. This can be hard, when our lives are so busy, but it is essential for our wellbeing. If you are at work, take a walk at lunchtime. At home, sneak off to the bathroom and wallow in the bath. Go outside and weed the garden, or sit and observe the wildlife.

By the time I arrive at the Excel Centre, I am open to analysis. I was missing the adventure supplied by my previous 3 year on the planet, and I was ready for anything. The beginning of the year had been pure hard work, planning for shows, running classes, building the business, and I was ready for a mini sabbatical.

Anthony Robbins is an American motivational speaker, personal finance instructor, and self-help author, who has the ability to hold his audience in the palm of his hand, for what seems like infinity. We were there at his invitation to 'Unleash the Power Within'. I had known all through my life that it was there; I just didn't know how to get it out. We arrive on the Friday morning, and go straight into a Seminar in the afternoon. His teaching is based on NLP: Neuro Linguistic Programming. Words are everything; especially the ones we use when talking to ourselves. I had hoped to have left my metaphorical shoulder monkey in Malta, but he somehow crept back into my suitcase, and had taken up residence in his favourite place, next to my right ear. If the dialogue with yourself consists of a constant stream of 'I can', ...then you can. Just knock the 't' off I can't and there you have it. Seemingly simples. The fire-walk we were about to undertake, was at the centre of our jaunt into enlightenment, and although apprehensive, I was ready for it. The fire-walk originated in Tibet, and Robbins uses it to great effect, to show us that if you can do something seemingly impossible – if you can walk on fire, then you can do anything. We spend the afternoon session being persuaded that what will be under out feet is not red hot coals, but cool moss. This takes time and is intense. A re-fashioning of the neural pathway, which tells us if we step on something red hot, we will burn ourselves. After four hours our bodies are consumed by empowering techniques, and with enabling words ringing in our ears, we find ourselves standing, along with 10,000 other people, in front of our goal.

We approach the awesome site of several 10ft runways of coals, heated to 1600 °C. Our task is to get from one end to the other without falling over, killing ourselves, becoming hysterical, or injuring another human being.

I am luckily by this time, in what Robbins describes as a 'Peak State'. If we change our body we change our state. Our physiology is directly linked to our emotional state. It is impossible to be down if your body language is up, and like everything, it's a choice. So I stand in a peak state, head up, chest out, with my re-fashioned neural pathway laid out before me. I am breathing deeply, and very importantly I have a fellow human with his hands placed firmly on my shoulders, while he whispers in my ear 'you can do this'. He has replaced the monkey, who has luckily gone for a tea break, and I am saying the same thing to the person in front. Just in case my brain and my neural pathways decided to go off at a tangent, there are marshals there to assess your state at the crucial moment, before you step onto the red hot coals.

I believe I can, and I do.

I leave the coals/cool moss behind me, and feel myself flying away from self-doubt. My new shoulder partner is long gone. Goodness knows where my friend is, I had lost her hours before; all I have is myself, 10,000 people, and a partly re-conditioned belief system.

There is an NLP technique called Anchoring. If you find yourself in 'a peak state' i.e. a state of happiness, joy, passion, self-belief, you can anchor yourself to this state, by touching an elbow, part of your arm, tapping your leg, etc. The idea is that when you need/wish to return to this state, you just need to touch the part of your body that you are anchored too. My belief, the one that told me that I could walk across the coals, and not burn my feet, was firmly anchored to my shoulders. I can still touch myself on either shoulder, and feel my body change instantly taking me back to that place of 'I can'.

Alice Hart-Davis, a journalist who was at the same event, wrote in *The Telegraph Magazine* on the 27th March, 2004, *'How does it work? I don't know. The theory is that your thoughts control your brain chemistry, and thus your body chemistry. Get yourself in the right state of mind and you are away. Sceptical physicists claim that the coals are a bad conductor of heat, so they are less likely to burn you – though plenty have sustained burns, including the odd physicist, trying to prove the bad conductor theory.'* Neither Alice nor I burnt our feet, but I am sure there were those that did, in-spite of the highly trained marshals.

I have used anchoring many times, when feeling self-doubt starting to creep in. But of course in the midst of trauma, stress, doubt, or anxiety these things can be forgotten, and the thought of being in a permanent 'peak state' actually leaves me feeling exhausted, so I use it sparingly! After all, we need downtime, we need opportunities to screw up, to be human, to fail. But when I need to do something, which is likely to catapult me out of my spotlight, and send me through the trap door into the darkness which exists under the stage, then I know that if I have the mind to, I can draw on my inner resources and get myself back into the light.

The fire-walk experience was a definite highlight of my Anthony Robbins weekend, but it was only Day 1, and the real work was still in front of me. When I awoke the next morning for Day 2 of my analytical adventure, I am faced with difficult questions. We are asked to identify five limiting beliefs, that have produced unwanted or negative consequences in our lives. I discover, as I pull my foundations down brick by brick, that the most disempowering belief that 'I am a mistake', is the cornerstone of my existence. The cornerstone (or foundation stone or setting stone), is the first stone set in the construction of a masonry foundation, important since all other stones will be set in reference to this stone, thus determining the position and strength of the entire structure.

The limiting beliefs that I am not attractive enough, not as intelligent as my brothers, whatever I do is not enough, and no man will love me, all go back to my foundations and the illusion that my mind has created. These and many others are built on top of my very wobbly corner stone. It is the contribution of conditioning. How can I be anything when I am a mistake? How can I be successful at what I do, how can I have a successful marriage? How can I successfully bring my children up? I was, it would appear playing a character that bore no resemblance to the real thing. I had donned a costume, taken up some props, and was in a play within a play. I had always, jokingly, been referred to as a mistake, having been born to my parents in their later years. I knew what a mistake was, due to the many mistakes made at school, and I knew that these were not good things as I was admonished for them. I had been absolved for the bad decisions I had made throughout my life, on a porch in Bosnia, but I had not forgiven myself for carrying around this false belief, which had caused such havoc during my time on the planet.

By the end of the weekend, and after a great deal of soul searching, and painful recollection, we take our dis-empowering beliefs up in an imaginary helicopter, to throw them out and explode them, turning them into dust. We replace them with empowering beliefs, a very important part of the whole process; beliefs that will act as building blocks on which we can stand securely and safely. Knowing that mistakes are not only ok, but a vital ingredient in our learning process turns me around, and I can see a path of progress, stretching out before me.

Having forgiven myself for holding on to these false beliefs, I go on to identify my passions, and try to clarify what I really want.

I want to make a difference.	I want my voice to be heard.
I want a soulmate.	I want enough money to travel.
I want to sing more.	I want to dance more.
I want to love more.	I want a house by the sea.

Many years later when reflecting on my childhood journey, I write the following, committing my leftover thoughts to paper. When we have dealt with emotional pain by facing it head on, which I had allowed myself to do at the Fire-walk Conference, we can effect a shift leaving space for the intellectualisation of the issue.

DIARY ENTRY
17th MAY, 2011 – ST LAWRENCE, ISLE OF WIGHT

Other people's daisy chains were much better than mine. I seemed to have trouble making the slits in the stems. They would tear leaving no alternative but for me to abandon them, and add them to a growing pile of casualties. The sight of the crestfallen flowers laying limp and without purpose induced a feeling of guilt. Bad enough that I had ripped them from their happy terrace, where they had spent the day dreaming and smiling back at the sun, I had then tossed them aside bringing their short lives to a rapid and unfulfilled close.

The problem was no fingernails. No nails, no slit, no chain, no crown. And boy did I want that crown. I thought if I had that on my head, the whole world would be at my feet; Queen of all

I surveyed. This of course was a crazy thing to think, given that my world was at that moment in time contained within a two up two down in Slough. But the world did lay at my feet; it's just that my head was telling me a different story. Layers and layers of thoughts and ideas, mostly other people's, made up tales about myself, and a newly emerging TV industry drew a picture, and formed a fragmented image which I rubbed out and re-drew on a daily basis. Hence no nails for slits due to my nervous nibbling.

Sitting in the middle of a field of daisies at the tender age of 10, on a sunny day, on my own, seemed like heaven. I needed nothing except the daisies and the grass, which was hosting its very own natural history programme. The ants were so good at being ants. Lying flat on your stomach, squinting with one eye, you could view them scuttling around, carrying things, focused and purposeful. It may have seemed chaotic, but they were doing stuff, kicking arse, making things happen. And as for the grass... Wow, such serenity of purpose, such elegance, such class. It was spectacularly good at, well just being grass really, providing a colourful and soft cushion, from where I could just sit and dream. But then I guess that's because the grass wasn't trying to be an ant. Even if it had tried really hard, it would have failed, given that it was the wrong colour and had no legs. I, on the other hand, spent my days thinking I needed to be more like my brothers, and less like me.

No one actually said that I did, I just always felt that I wasn't quite up to the job of being me. I felt as if something was missing. It didn't help being plonked on the back kitchen table having my auburn locks cut into brotherly conformity, because to be fair it had worked for them, so why wouldn't it work for me? I hadn't read Freud back then, so the idea that I may have 'penis envy' didn't cross my mind, although to this day I can, when I allow myself to, still feel distressed by the fact that my poor parents, who were stuck in their own post-war time warp, would have been better off with another boy. Bad enough that I was a girl, but I was constantly referred to as a mistake.

When I was born in 1953, having boys was far more useful than girls. If needed they could fight wars, and save the world again, should such another terror arise out of the mist. Us girls on the other hand were just supposed to get married, stay in the kitchen, and look after the children. But I somehow got caught in the crossfire of the 1950s. The volcanic reaction of post war women, thrown back into the home to make way for the returning male, after feeling such equality outside the kitchen, hadn't quite fully ignited. They had, like my daisies being tossed aside, and were heading for an unfulfilling exit. So there I was, learning how to cook omelettes, sew, and iron serviettes the correct way, which I now do with aplomb; and as you know you can't beat a perfectly ironed serviette. I took up my place at the back of the Maths class and I hid. Even if I'd had the courage to speak up, Mr Gaskell would have scowled at me so badly, I would have had to rub myself out and start yet again.

Years later, unable to fight my apparent intelligence, and sitting in the back of my university lecture hall, along with the other 'mature students' who had escaped from the ironing board, I recalled pulling the petals from the daisies. Loves me, loves me not, loves me, loves me not. I know now that my parents loved me, my father more than my mother probably; but that's ok. She was left in hospital verging on death, after giving birth to me prematurely, having made it through a war, two war babies, the death of a child, and an apparently torturous time caring for her mother, who was dying from cancer. My conception was not planned. It was a mistake. My eldest brother was 19 years older than me, leaving home the minute I was born. It must have felt like a very heavy cross to bear becoming pregnant once again, just as her life was just becoming easier. Electric shock therapy and tranquillisers were something out of my sphere of understanding. I just wanted to be loved.

I carried my own cross for a very long time through 3 marriages, to which I clung to for my needs to be met, my wrongs to be righted and for my problems to be solved. I tried each time to be someone different. The first mask didn't work, neither did the next one, nor the next. So after playing the wrong part, on the wrong stage for decades, I have decided to just be me, warts, and all. I have stopped trying to push that last rather large daisy head through a small fragile hole in order to make a crown, and instead, cherish every wonderful moment of being me, someone I am actually starting to like.

I left the Seminar hoping that the Power Within Me, having seen a break in the clouds, would rise up and all would be well. But the energy of the 4 year, which can feel hard and full of obstacles, had not quite finished with me. After all it was only March.

The summer holidays come around, and I decide to take my youngest daughter on a trip to Hartlepool, finishing with a week in Wales with a school friend and her mum. I have often talked about Hartlepool with affection, but my children only know of the place where I was born, Slough, and the place where their grandparents lived. But my parents had moved down from Hartlepool in the depression, and settled where there was work.

My eldest brother was born there, and until recently, I thought that my other brother had been born there too, but he wasn't. My mind had been playing tricks on me, and had managed to turn correct information into incorrect information; these illusions had left me feeling displaced. My sense of home was confused and distorted, as everyone seemed to come from where I didn't. The ground beneath my feet felt like shifting sand; not the best substance to try and build foundations on. We had an annual pilgrimage back to the North to visit family and friends, and I so wanted to dispel the idea that I was a mistake, that for many years I lied about my beginnings, telling everyone back in Slough that I had been born in Hartlepool too. The lie, as lies do, had become a burden, anchoring me to a place where true expression would always allude me. I'm sure to other people it made no difference where I came from, but to me it meant everything.

My diary entries of the visit with my daughter, chart the journey to geographical acceptance, and freedom from an obstacle which had continued to plague me for many years. Wherever you are on your journey, foundational issues are something which will keep rising to the surface, until they have been addressed. The 4 Personal Year energy will help you untangle the bindings if you are willing to step into the space. I can't tell you why, but my experience assures me that it will.

…Coincidently the trip ran over my parents' birthdays – my mother being born on the 8th of August and my father on the 16th. Maybe synchronicity was the coincidence.

DIARY ENTRY
SUNDAY 8th AUGUST, 2004 – YORK

Arrived in York to bright sunshine and searing heat. Took the 'park and ride' into the City which was packed with Sunday tourists. The Minster was hosting a service to commemorate the D-Day Landings, and ex-service personnel complete with ice creams, hats, and medals, took their places on the city's benches, enjoying the afternoon sun. It was the day of my Dad's birthday, and I wondered whether he had ever stood in the same spot as we were standing, gazing up at the magnificent Minster. It is a beautiful Gothic-style church, designed to be the greatest cathedral in the kingdom. It took around 250 years to build between 1220 and 1472 and stands solidly and confidently, whilst the bustle of the everyday life continues all around it. York had been mentioned many times in my childhood, but mostly in connection with the famous racecourse, a place where my father had felt completely at home.

DIARY ENTRY
MONDAY 9th AUGUST, 2004 – YORK

We breakfast in the strangely resplendent dining room at the Ramada Jarvis. My daughter informs me that the Japanese are taking over the world as three leave the dining room. The crowd of Germans from the previous evening had eaten early and left without a trace. Morning again in York, and we gain entry to the Minster. It is overwhelming. Its Gothic arches reach up to the heavens and into the silence, leaving the visitors far below. I light a candle in memory of my Dad, and leave feeling content. We had not been able to gain entry yesterday, due to the service, but it was worth the wait. The weather draws in as we leave York and head up the A1 to Scotch Corner, another name etched in my mind. The A1 is jammed with lorries. By the time we reach the Farmers Arms Public House at Catterick Bridge, the rain is pouring down. We make our way to Richmond and spend the afternoon reminiscing with my cousin Joan the former Landlady of the Farmers Arms. We talk about her father, my Uncle Tommy, and the old days. Joan is struggling with her hip, her knee, and gout, just like Uncle Tommy. An occupational hazard perhaps when one is a member of the Licensed Victuallers trade. Later that day we arrive at Seaton Carew, Hartlepool. It is still raining, and make our way to the Marine Hotel – the memories slowly start to flood my consciousness.

After a supper of scampi and chips, we take a tour, heading for the old town. I am keen to reacquaint myself. Amazingly after 40 years it is fresh in my mind; the bits that haven't changed beyond all recognition that is. Past the football stadium and out to the Headland. The Fish Sands beacon flashes as always, as St Hilda's still stands grey and silent against the darkening horizon. I am filled with a strange sensation, as I stand where the people of the town, as legend had it, hung a monkey, mistaken for a French Spy, over 200 years ago during the Napoleonic Wars. I wonder what had been so romantic about this slither of the East Coast as a child. My roots had tried to grow into the sand, refusing to accept the many wrenchings back to the south, trying to cling on to something which felt secure.

I still love this place, and tears fill my eyes as I peer across the North Sea, to the grey horizon beyond. Friar Street and Ingram House beckon, my mind failing me a little, as I drive around the headland in search of the memory of Aunt Edna. She and Uncle Tommy are long gone, but in my mind's eye, she is still there, making me eat my greens, serving ice cold milk, and fighting her corner. Uncle Tommy is still at the Park Hotel chatting to the customers and holding court.

Our beds beckon as we make our way back past The Victoria Ground, Hartlepool United's home and a place where I had spent many a Saturday afternoon. I sleep fitfully, memories invading my repose.

DIARY ENTRY
TUESDAY 10th AUGUST, 2004 – HARTLEPOOL

It's raining, but the freshly cooked breakfast revives our spirits, which are a little soggy from the inclemency of the North East summer. We are heading to the doctors just around the corner. I always resist going to the doctors, but since arriving in Hartlepool, every joint in my body has started to hurt and it is a struggle just putting one foot in front of the other. An appointment is made for 3.20 and we carry on with our day. On our arrival back at the doctors, after another day of reminiscing in the rain, I am told there is nothing to be found. But I feel shaken to my roots. It is as if my joints want to disentangle themselves from each other, screaming for release. We make our way to the Museum of Hartlepool, and I am distracted. Old photos, stories, names mentioned time and time again throughout my life, jump off the page making me feel at one with the familiar.

Church Street, Lynn Street, Burn Valley Gardens, St Hilda's Church. The museum is followed by a trip back to Hartlepool United. We are shown around the ground, by a passionate groundsman, although I think the only thing he is passionate about is the grass (which of course is the perfect thing to be passionate about, if you are a groundsman)!

We have just missed Jo who has swept the floor for 50 years, and would no doubt have remembered Tommy Aird, my mother's brother, who was Chairman of the club for a period. I remember the wooden fence and benches, now replaced by fearsome looking iron railings to keep the fans in, and the troublemakers out. We are shown the changing rooms, and the players walkway is pulled out so we may walk onto the pitch. I feel honoured to set foot in a place so ingrained in my childhood memories, and which clearly means the world to our guide. It is his Wembley.

The night before, when we had driven to the Fish Sands, my past had rushed before my eyes, and when the rushing stopped, we were greeted with a grey unwelcoming image of chimneys which form the industrial landscape further along the coast. They were there in my childhood, but I didn't see them. We had returned to the Borough Hall in search of Uncle Tommy's Mayoral picture, which is apparently on the wall, inextricably linked to Hartlepool's history, but it is closed. Our trip to the town centre reveals a sorry sight. No more Binns, that wonderful Department store where we dressed up and went for afternoon tea. I felt very happy there. The beautiful building is now a nightclub, and is faced by distasteful plastic signs heralding the fact. I manage to navigate to Park Road and the Park Hotel, which is now called the Park Inn. Once again the memories hit me like a truck. We go in and explain the nature of our visit. The place has just had a re-fit and is no longer The Park Hotel I remember. But the smell is still there and as it hits my nostrils and courses through my fragile body I feel a sense of home. It is not a pleasant smell, but as with all smells, it evokes strong memories.

The wool shop opposite remains. The old lady and her sister who used to let me help out are long gone, but the daughter is now firmly installed behind the same wooden counter. I had spent many happy hours feeling very grown up, valued and responsible in that shop, serving customers and tidying up.

I buy some wool to make a jumper which I no doubt will never finish, let alone wear. My daughter is tasked with making a child's dress for a school project, and we buy a pattern, material, scissors, pins, and cotton. I spend as much as I can; times are clearly hard in Hartlepool. Part payment on a debt gratitude is repaid.

DIARY ENTRY
WEDNESDAY 11th AUGUST, 2004 – TELFORD

As we make our way out of Hartlepool, the sun comes out and the pain in my body inexplicably starts to subside. I have collected the missing part of my soul which I had left on the Fish Sands, and have left another part of me there. I'm not sure what it is, but I think it will be there for ever.

The north moors twinkle in the summer sun, and I start to relax, but our arrival in Skipton is fraught with traffic jams and pedestrians. It would seem like the whole of Yorkshire is here. We eventually park, head for the market, and purchase two green chairs to aid us in our attempts at watercolour. The next day we make our way further South.

DIARY ENTRY
THURSDAY 12th AUGUST, 2004 – TELFORD

The drive to Telford is long and boring, and broken only by a short stop at another uninspiring service station. When we arrive at the Telford Golf and Country Club, we are greeted by hailstones. A swim in the pool and soak in jacuzzi revives us, and we are ready for action. Eating action. We blow the budget, and spend a satisfying evening in the restaurant overlooking the splendid

Gorge. Looking forward to seeing Ironbridge tomorrow – a place I have always wanted to go to.

DIARY ENTRY
FRIDAY 13th AUGUST, 2004 – TELFORD

We walk along the towpath, and imagine living in one of the beautiful cottages which line the side of the gorge. We have crossed the bridge, which is an awesome sight, and just in case they are not completely gone, I recall my recently identified disempowering beliefs, and mentally hurl them into the gorge. It feels very good, although our trip to Hartlepool has thrown me, and I am consumed by a renewed feeling of displacement. As I stand in the middle of the bridge I imagine myself as a depository of accumulated wisdom. A facilitator: a place where people can walk from one side to the other, collecting a few snippets of enlightenment, before reaching the other side. The industrial age started here in Ironbridge, and there is a surreal feeling about the place. The visitors are sparse as we make our way to the Gorge Museum. Technology has moved forward but the past is not forgotten. I am fascinated. The place feels so solid. The bridge has a beautiful and eerie strength about it. Clearly it will be there for many years to come. I hold on to my vision of 'Bridge Buddy' as we make our way to the other side and back to our hotel.

I leave my daughter tacking her darts (having explained to her about short cuts); I might like to take them, but not sure I want my daughter to. I make my way outside with my newly acquired watercolours and painting chair. The sun has at last come out, and I spend a peaceful two hours attempting to improve my painting technique. The addition of grey to my palette helps, and

I attempt patience as I try to paint the wall, starting brick by brick from the bottom up.

DIARY ENTRY
MONDAY 16th AUGUST, 2004 – WALES

We have arrived in Wales and receive a warm welcome from our friends. Unfortunately, I feel as if I have been run over by a bus and my body is once again screaming at me. The distance over the week was over 800 miles. York, Catterick, Hartlepool, Skipton, Telford, Bridge North, Shrewsbury. We arrive on what would have been my Mum's birthday, and for some reason this anniversary is buzzing around my mind. The mattress on my bed in the tiny cottage is full of lumps, and after lying on it for ten minutes, in order to recover myself a little, I decide to ask the owner if it is possible to change it. This is done, and I congratulate myself on speaking up as I lay back down on a much improved mattress.

I am still struggling to process all the stuff from our trip to Hartlepool, but today things become clearer, as I make an effort to release myself from the big divide. I stand beneath the gothic arch of what is left of Talley Abbey. It is in the field adjacent to the cottage we are renting, and it has been calling me there over the past 24 hours. I reason with myself. I am a Gemini – it is a dual sign and there are two of me. Of course I can come from both places. I spot a sign close to where I am standing, which translates the name of the place written in Welsh into English. The meaning when translated from the Welsh is 'two lakes'. I stand with the wind blowing in my hair and ask the Universe to help unshackle me. As I look around, the beauty of the place seeps into my body, as I determine to re-build the mental landscape which has floored me so many times. I giggle as an image comes into my mind of a flamingo stood on one leg. I place my feet firmly on the ground balanced astride the cornerstones of my past, and imagine long silver roots anchoring me to a place of safety and love; a place where duality is a source of strength. The wind dies down and I feel at one with everything. It is a very spiritual experience.

The next day we visit a healer in the town, and Reiki is administered, leaving me tired, but further along the path to feeling at least some degree of wellbeing. The sea calls and we head for the coast. Serendipity steps in, and due to an unexpected diversion we end up in Aberaeron. My brother had been the landlord of a public house here called the Harbourmaster, which I had visited with my son and eldest daughter many years previously. He had his own family demons, and had sadly drunk the place, and himself into a state of bankruptcy. My father had tried to fit him into the same hole as his elder brother, and had pushed him into an apprenticeship. But he was a square peg, and ended up damaged by trying to fit into a round hole. He had alluded to this many times, like a mantra. My elder brother found success and satisfaction as a leader and businessman, putting his Engineering Apprenticeship to good use. But my other brother lost his way. He was a highly talented writer and musician, achieving some success in later life, but never really managed to stay in the spotlight. The Harbourmaster had finally fallen into disrepair and he had left. When we arrive at Aberaeron, quite by chance, as we had been diverted there on our way to somewhere else, it is once again pouring down with rain. I recognise the name, and ask if I can jump out and walk along the esplanade, to see if the pub is around the corner. I leave my travelling companions in the car, and make my way in what I think is the right direction. I am met on the short walk by a bedraggled and sad looking woman who stops and talks to me. She is sad because she is on this side of the water in Wales, and her family is on the other side of the water in Cork.

She tells me that her parents brought her here many years ago, and had eventually moved back to Cork. She had remained here. She tells me that she feels as if she has been left at a bus stop. I recognise the synchronicity and hug her. I tell her my story, and recall the past few days and I can see that this brings her immense comfort. When you feel displaced, you can feel like the only person in the world who understands. Due to the rain I am about to return to the car, but as she bids me farewell she urges me to continue my search for the Harbourmaster. I carry on a little further and when I turn, she is gone. A few more metres and I am faced with the Harbour. In that very moment, the sun came out and the rain ceased, as if by magic. I am stopped dead in my tracks as I gaze upon the Harbourmaster. It is beautifully painted in a deep shade of blue, and is bedecked with pots of vibrant flowers. I go back and collect the rest of the party and suggest lunch. I ask my friend if she had seen the woman. She had seen no-one. We go in for a drink and a pub lunch, and I ask if I can be shown round, having told them that my brother was a previous owner. They gladly oblige. I look at the newspaper cuttings on the wall showing the awards for the building and restoration, and I am inspired at what 'can be done'. The lesson is loud and clear.

I'm not sure how I feel about the idea of angels, but to this day I still believe that the woman on the seafront was sent to me in an hour of crisis, so that I could help her. By helping her, I helped myself, and made a difference to another human being through my story. This filled my heart with joy, and I felt that all the pain I had suffered was there to be used in some way, for the purpose of teaching.

I return home to face the remainder of the year. In spite of all the amazing progress this year had brought me, it had also brought me to my knees. It has not been easy – I had felt well below par, and in a great deal of pain. My joints, my muscles, my lungs, and my heart all ached. A large chunk of my past has been revisited, relived, and finally reconciled, and I felt released from the grip imposed by my consciousness. Now to rebuild my body.

I construct a strategy to improve my wellbeing. I am willing to try anything and choose homeopathy, acupuncture, and hypnosis. They all work in harmony allowing my revived spirit to act as cement, giving me the strength to move some new foundation stones into place. But I'm not quite there yet.

Whatever Personal Year you are in when you reach September, you will be given a double dose of the energy, and push towards the Right Action demanded by the year, before being drawn towards the following year's focus. It is the time to harvest the lessons of the year.

DIARY ENTRY
21st SEPTEMBER, 2004 – ASCOT

I take a bath and unexpectedly become extremely upset. I ask the Universe for help. I start breathing deeply in and out, and enter a strange dream-like state, where I visualise the word rejection coming out of my mouth on my out breaths. An avalanche of the word follows forming a huge bonfire. I see myself walking to get a lighted torch to help it set the pile on fire, and I stand watching as it burns to ashes. I was careful to make sure it had burned completely. As I let the bathwater out, I imagine that it is extinguishing the burning embers.

Sitting on the bed with my head in a towel looking in the mirror, I remembered an incident in the hairdressers when my Mum died. Whilst waiting for the stylist with a towel wrapped around my head, I had looked up to see my mother's face staring back at me. I wanted to say something, but I had no words. It was in the first year of university, and she had died halfway through my exams. For some reason I felt compelled to get my hair done. I look in the mirror again, and this time find some words. I tell her how much her rejection had hurt me and how much pain it had caused. My throat tightens and I become unable to talk further, the words I need to say getting stuck in my throat. A few days later I visit a lovely gentle alternative practitioner, and recall the events of the past few days. She uses some alternative therapy to clear my heart and throat chakras, which are apparently blocked. I feel yet another enormous shift. I return home and disappear into a deep sleep.

A friend comes for lunch the next day, and by chance she is a hypnotherapist. I start to tell her about the last 48 hours, and ask her if she would see me at some stage and take me back on a timeline, to see if I can clear some more of the pain. She did it there and then.

No time like the present apparently.

Lying on my settee I feel a huge ball of something coming towards me, and I desperately try to move backwards... I realise that it is LOVE and I am terrified of it. I am rejecting it before it can reject me. This is a huge surprise to me, despite the fact that it is so obvious. It is a hugely emotional experience, but I am in good hands. I understand in that moment, that I had been blocking love all my life. Scared to fully give, and terrified of receiving. There is foundational rubble all around me, and the pain is far worse than trending on Lego blocks. But something has shifted, and the opportunity is there to start to 're-build'.

My very difficult and emotional 4 year ends with a tsunami; a real one. My daughter who is travelling in the area misses it by days. My son who has recently returned from Iraq, is there to comfort me, along with my youngest daughter and his girlfriend, now his wife. I am so grateful to have most of my family in one place, and can only hope that my daughter will be safe, and eventually return to the fold. It had been an enormously trying year, but I had survived.

At FASBAT we had been producing an Old Time Music Hall. This is constructed using several different acts, which are glued together by a chairman who oversees the proceedings. Acrobats, singers, magicians, comedians and dancers all rehearse their pieces separately, and form the building blocks for the show. As I watch the show materialise before my eyes, I can see the effectiveness of this genre, and the strength provided by the separate blocks, which made it one of our most successful productions ever. We were to use the format again and again with both adults and children.

Obstacles and limitations are two of the words associated with the 4 energy, and I had reached the end of my 4 Personal Year, feeling as if I had overcome many. They had been standing in my way of progress, alongside the rather large elephant which had taken up all the space in my new ideas and possibilities box. The elephant had been dismembered bit by bit, and the limitations I had placed upon myself from childhood, had dissipated. I was ready for some new adventures.

The last entry in my diary, is a phrase I had picked up from somewhere during my year-long journey.

DIARY ENTRY
31st DECEMBER, 2004

ALL DIFFICULTIES ARE FOR THE PURPOSE OF GROWTH.

YEAR 5:
THE FREE SPIRIT, AGENT OF CHANGE

Keywords: Flexibility · Freedom · Discipline

Underbalanced	**Right Action**	*Overbalanced*
inactive		*impatient*
unsure		*impulsive*
passionless	EXPANSION	*unreliable*
cautious	EXPLORATION	*reckless*
ineffective	VERSATILITY	*overactive*
	INDEPENDENCE	*thrill-seeking*
	TRAVEL	
	FLOW	

USE FREEDOM PRODUCTIVELY

CHARACTER BRIEF
Risk-taking explorer looking for adventure

Costume	**Props**
Catsuit of Change	Airline Ticket
Free Spirit Fleece	Running Shoes
Versatility Vest	Can of Curiosity

■ 5555555555555555555 ■

YEAR 5:

TO THE OTHER SIDE

AND BACK AGAIN

Don't fence me in. The 5 loves freedom and wants to come and go as it pleases. See how the number is open at both sides. It is so adaptable, likes so much variety, that it sometimes doesn't know if it is coming or going. Pythagoras called the 5 'Masculine and Feminine', for it is composed of 2 and 3. 5 is very popular and gets along very well with both men and women. Because 5 is not bound-in like the confining square of 4, it is apt to take chances, be the daredevil. It has no fear, wants new experiences; is willing to gamble.

Shirley Blackwell Lawrence MSc. D
The Secret Science of Numerology

As I enter January 2005, I still have the warm fuzzy feeling, produced by my son coming to comfort me when the news of the tsunami broke, and the knowledge that my eldest daughter, having narrowly avoided the tsunami, is happily continuing her time travelling. This, plus the lingering enjoyment of spending quality time with my youngest daughter over the summer, all adds up to my feeling of family. However, I stand at the beginning of a new year with an urge to explore, and decide to put family matters aside for a while and turn towards myself.

I always describe the number 5 using my fingers. If you imagine your fingers all stuck together in a 4 year, which is more akin to the earthy Taurus or cautious Capricorn energy, in a 5 year it is as if the glue has dissolved and they are suddenly free, giving the possibility of expansion and change. This energy has far more in common with Gemini and Sagittarius. There are of course dangers to look out for, such as scattered energy and overindulgence, and it would seem that these are always waiting in the wings, ready to upstage you. I often refer to the 5 as the sex and drugs and rock and roll number, as so many rock stars are in cahoots with this number. I have suffered from scattered energy all my life, and this has on many occasions scuppered any advances I had made. I am an ideas person and my head likes to go off in different directions, darting around all over the place looking for new things, collecting information and turning it into an endless dialogue of incessant chattering. This can be very tiring for all involved, including me, and if you don't harness the energy, you can spend your time getting nowhere.

The first thing I noticed about the start of my 5 year, was that I had itchy feet, and they were keen to dance around on a different stage; the one I had started to construct in my 4 year. Those new foundations felt different; they didn't feel as if they were about to collapse with the weight of my old belief system. Something had definitely shifted, and although they were not yet strong enough to withstand major earthquakes, it definitely felt like a start. I decide I should try a nice slow waltz before hurling myself into a full on can can, so I start my dance close to home on London's South Bank. I always find joy jumping on a train, sitting back, and arriving in the metropolis. I am wearing my catsuit of change, and I'm ready for anything. Bring it on, I want it all. The sex, the drugs, and the rock and roll. My free spirit fleece is wrapped around me (which is just as well as it's jolly cold), and I am ready to explore.

The South Bank is such an explosion of expression. The chatter of the crowd, eager to enjoy the offers of culture contained within the walls of the National Theatre, The Royal Festival Hall, the Tate, the Globe, and the National Film Theatre fills me with excitement, and I want to soak it all in.

The 5 Personal Year energy is adaptable, dynamic, excitable, and curious, and if you find yourself with lots of odd numbers in your chart, like me, you will probably be very adept at being at one with it. However, one of the challenges for the even numbers in a 5 year is flow. It is about learning to adapt to changing circumstances; and this may be something you balk against. If there is one thing we can rely on in life, it is change, and the 5 is the number in which circumstances can go from good to bad, bad to good, and back again. It sits at the centre of the 9 year Epicycle, and can be seen as a balancing point.

As I walk along the South Bank heading towards the Tate Modern, my destination for the day, I am drawn towards an advert for a Mime Festival. I buy a ticket and take the ride. It is a show exploring time and space, real and imagined, and I am sucked into the whole question of reality. What is it? Do I live in the world, or is the world living in me? I think I like the idea of the world living in me. The idea of living in the world seems so fixed and limiting right at this moment, and I feel myself being drawn towards a much bigger picture.

Looking down from the cafe at the top of the Tate across to St Paul's, I gaze upon the hordes of people walking across the millennium bridge. The skyline stands majestically in the background, leaving the inhabitants looking like ants, scurrying around getting on with their daily business. I am mesmerised. It's as if I am in an installation. One of those arty, mind altering installations in a small dark room, where reality merges with unreality, leaving you feeling rather displaced. Having had my coffee fix, and sitting as long as I can just gazing out and pondering my existence, I reluctantly move on. It's a busy place; people stare at your empty coffee cup. They know nothing of your struggle. I wonder would they be less eager to grab your seat if they knew what was going on in your head? Maybe they need the same fix. Go with the flow, go with the flow.

I find myself standing in front of a Mondrian; a non-figurative painting – planes of primary colour with black and white – they convey what he described as a 'dynamic equilibrium', which he hoped would work on the individual spirit, and have wider social implications. Well it certainly had an effect on me. My 5 year invites me to spread my wings, take a risk, push the boundaries, and go with the flow. But as I stand and gaze at the neat boxes, they give me a feeling of security, and I am torn between the joy of fear, and the fear of safety. So there's the rub.

No matter how much you crave freedom in a 5 year, and of course it is easy to think of freedom as a ditching of certain things, or a bolt in a different direction, perhaps towards a more hedonistic lifestyle; it is important to hang on to the things gained in the previous first four years of the cycle. You need to know what it is serves you, and then you need to hang on to it. You need to consider the progress you have made so that you can build on it. One theme of the 5 year is to find freedom through discipline. I have so often been on the verge of something which has become rather hard, and have chosen to throw it in the bin rather than stick with it. This has never resulted in freedom. It has generally resulted in more dissatisfaction, and in some cases entrapment. But the 5 Personal Year is also a time to explore, and push the boundaries of ideas which have been dreamt up, which is why it is the number of travel and adventure.

This doesn't need to be physical, as it can all be done using your mind's eye. However, if you can travel, you will always find that this opens the mind. Anthony Bourdain, the American celebrity chef and travel writer said, 'Travel isn't always pretty. It isn't always comfortable. Sometimes it hurts, it even breaks your heart. But that's okay. The journey changes you; it should change you. It leaves marks on your memory, on your consciousness, on your heart, and on your body. You take something with you. Hopefully, you leave something good behind.'

The art I am encountering is having a powerful effect on me and has my head travelling back to all the significant moments in my life, whilst I try to make sense of my current state. It is opening up my mind to all sorts of business ideas which can be built on. This is in stark contrast to the deconstructive feel of my previous year.

Christian Boltanski is my next Tate treat.

'The Swiss are naturally healthy and yet dying all the time' reads the caption on the wall. Photos of dying cells confirm this cheerful statement, as I gaze at the installation of 42 photographic portraits of men woman and children of varying ages. Electric lamps are clipped to the top edge of each frame, and bent down to direct the light on to the faces of those portrayed.

The photographs were appropriated by the artist from obituaries published in *Le Nouvelliste du Valais*, a provincial Swiss newspaper. Boltanski amassed these clippings over several years, and selected the portraits at random from his collection. The artist then re-photographed the already grainy images and had enlarged prints produced, so that the heads are slightly bigger than life-size. The identity of the subjects is obliterated by the poor quality of the resulting prints and the removal of any accompanying memorial text from the obituary. Regarding his presentation of these individuals, Boltanski stated, 'I suppose part of the work is also about the simple fascination of seeing somebody who is handsome and imagining his ashes' (Boltanski in Rainbird and Boltanski, 1993; page 4).

I am reminded that life is not only short, but precious. I already look as old as some of the images, and I am not quite ready for my ashes to be flung of the top of some mountain or planted under a tree. If I am to spread my wings and seek out new opportunities, I need to do it soon whilst I feel the urge. I hoped I could hang on to the bits of myself that work, and use them as a springboard from which to leap into my future.

Lunch beckons and I am greeted by the sounds of a Gipsy violin and accordion player in the lobby of the National Theatre, playing with such life and movement which fuels my desire even further. The programme informs me that the violinist is 70, and the accordion player is 30. I could feel their music vibrating through them and their instruments, as they musically danced around with each other; talent, age, and expression enabling them to meld into one. I feel the stage, the walls, the floor, and the audience all resonating in harmony, completely filling the space; everything is connected to everything else, flowing in the moment. This wonderful realisation of the complete connectivity of the universe, works its way into my head, and I feel as if I am starting to understand more of everything. The Pythagorean view of the universe as a living, harmonic mixture is alive and well in this very moment. As I sit in a microcosm of maths and music I feel completely whole.

The freedom I feel during my trip to the big city continues, and focuses my mind on what freedom actually means for me. I definitely want to hold on to the ideas created in my 3 year, and the new empowering beliefs I had dreamt up in my 4 year. These were held firmly in my mind and heart and I wasn't about to ditch them anytime soon. But there was one particular thing in my 5 year that I definitely needed freedom from, and this was physical.

My ex-husband had bought me a piano. This arrived in the December, and he left my life in January.

I am now housed in the flat I purchased specifically to accommodate the piano, which is starting to feel like a heavy weight around my neck. I just can't get away from it. It is very large, and unlike the elephant I encountered in Chapter 4, I am unable to take it apart piece by piece in order to understand the separate components, deal with it and move on.

No, it just sits there refusing to move. Before I had made the move to the flat, a close and caring friend had advised me to get rid of it. She could clearly see that I was looking for a house to home the piano, rather than a house to create a home. But she wasn't a musician, and didn't really understand the joy that the shiny black Yamaha Baby Grand oozed from every inch of its sexy little body. One of the things I am is a musician, not a top notch professional one, but a musician all the same. The piano arrived after my Grade 5 success, and I had every hope of continuing on to Grade 6. I actually believed it would make me play better; but of course it was only practise that was going to achieve that. All it actually gave me was a pain in the neck, both physically and mentally. When you play an upright piano the music is right in front of your eyes. With a baby grand you need to look upward to read the music, and this I found physically taxing. I had lost the impetus to do my Grade 6, and my heart still hurt. I had also lost the will to have it staring me in the face, reminding me of the series of events that had led to my singular life, every time I walked into the lounge. It had to go.

Luckily, some friends had recently moved to a rather grand house in the country, and were looking for somewhere to put their collection of silver framed pictures. The piano fitted the bill and they promised to cherish it, dust it, and make sure that the children were given the opportunity to play it, and so I released myself from the torture, receiving a handsome sum in the process. All in all a very painful experience, which would eventually turn into a blessing. As soon as it is out of my sight I start to hatch a plan with what to do with the money.

I would re-do the bathroom, buy a work of art and travel. I have my best ideas lying in a bath, and the old stained Victorian iron bath, currently hiding in the corner of my bathroom wasn't coming up with the goods. At the beginning of February, during an unexpected trip to Scotland, I buy a beautiful watercolour from a friend of a friend.

Charles Jamieson trained at the Glasgow School of Art and I love the vibrancy of his work. He travels widely, capturing the essence of his locations in his pared back landscapes. I find the picture hanging on the artists wall at his home, during a visit with my travelling companion. The painting is waiting to go to an exhibition in London, having been painted during a trip to a Greek island. It has a sun bleached road disappearing around a corner into the unknown. It touches my soul, and I make the purchase. It now acts as a constant reminder that none of us know what is round the corner, and that learning to go with the flow is a very useful tool to have in your box of tricks. I'm on a roll, and suggest to my youngest daughter that we take a trip to Australia and New Zealand, planning to catch up with her sister who is travelling, post university. She is missing her terribly and jumps at the chance. There is also a cousin in New Zealand to visit, and her sister is very fortuitously there over the Easter holidays. Suddenly, right before me, I can see an adventure, a big adventure and this feels very good. The seven 5s in my chart are dancing around all over the place, and can hardly contain themselves.

I entered my 5 year not only longing for a sense of adventure, but also an expansion of my mind. I had been reading about Socrates and I'm taken by the fact the he wandered around Athens in a shabby cloak hiding a very fit body. He proposed that in order to live 'the good life', we need to consider body, mind, and soul. At this stage, my body was not exactly honed, my mind was confused, and my soul was still searching, but I wondered whether philosophy might ease some of my discontent, and provide some much needed answers. With the flights booked and some free time ahead of me once again the expansive energy of the number 5, sees me heading off into the unknown, and the Philosophical Society of England.

They meet just off Sloane Square, and I am very excited.

DIARY ENTRY
MONDAY 7th MARCH, 2005 – LONDON

There is a beggar sitting in the cold March air and I give him a pound coin. I wanted to talk to him about the meaning of life, but I didn't. Would that be more beneficial than a pound? A chance to explore life through Socratic discourse. Pizza Express, Sloane Square, provides a warm retreat for a late lunch. I may not have strayed far from Ascot, but already I feel like a world traveller. The basement is full of glamorous and vibrant young people, and there is a real buzz. I mostly like peace and quiet, but today I am after something different. Someone drops a beer on the floor and just leaves it. As they came into the restaurant it seemed as if they had too much of everything to live in spirit. Oh how I judge. But I had recently read of a man who had millions, several houses, and beautiful gardens. He speaks of his spiritual journey, and his sense of relief when he downsizes to a small flat and a bonsai tree... but of course that's just his journey, and not everyone is on that same bus. But I want to know, who is happier – the man on the street or the children of wealthy parents. Is there a centre-ground? If I had the courage I would go back and talk to the man on the street.

Funny... I thought I had courage.

What am I afraid of?

· Offending him? No
· Looking odd? No
· Not hearing what I want to hear? ...possibly
· Feeling helpless? Yes

The meeting of the Philosophical Society is held at The Antelope in Eton Place, and is stimulating, enlightening, flirty, fun, and creative, in spite of the fact that there are only ten people in attendance. The Philosophical Society of England seems like a rather grand title, given the amount of people present and I ponder whether thinking is on the decline.

DIARY ENTRY
TUESDAY 8th MARCH, 2005 – ASCOT

Eleven days to go and I am sitting drinking coffee, after one of the best nights of my life (so far anyway). I LOVE Philosophy – I do declare I am a Philosopher! I will miss the next session 'The Philosophy of Mathematics'. Probably not a bad thing, as memories of Mr Gaskell throwing the board rubber at me, as I was trying to hide at the back of the Maths class, permeate my mind. But I'm guessing that the philosophical discussion will be so much more than 2 + 2 = 4. Now that does sound interesting!

As I ready myself to leave, on what I hope will be the adventure of a lifetime, the temptation to pack more in my rucksack is overwhelming. This is juxtaposed with the feeling that however much I take will be too much. I want to be free of baggage of every sort: emotional, financial, physical, spiritual. In New Zealand I want to gaze at the stars, meditate on the beach, and come to who I am. Am I anywhere close yet? I have no idea. I wonder if there something on the other side of the world for me which isn't here, or will I be like the boy in The Alchemist, and realise that I have travelled all that way to find that everything I need is within myself?

I pen the following questions.
   Is my soulmate there?
   Is my soulmate a country?
   Is my soulmate me?

Good questions, Miss Flynn.

I pick up an abandoned newspaper in the cafe to accompany my daily fix, and turn to the horoscopes...

Do countries abroad represent real opportunities for you? This is a question that you will soon have to answer. In truth the grass may really be greener on the other side of the world. But have you considered that it is not. Could it be that a dream of working abroad is a convenient explanation for dissatisfaction that you feel at work? It is important that you solve this riddle as you will soon be making some key decisions that depend on your answer.

I had told the Universe I wanted to get 'philosophical', and it would seem it was providing me with lots of questions. Really... a horoscope, on that day, at that moment, in that place. Wow.

I had recently discovered that my Life Path Number is a 7, the number of the Analyst, the Seeker of Truth; and I was starting to get a feel for the fact that I loved the philosophic discipline. I love being a hermit, with time to think and analyse. In fact I was starting to realise that I quite like being in my own company. Suddenly things started to make more sense. I take myself back to the apple tree in the back garden of my youth, and recall how happy I was sitting securely in its branches, thinking about stuff. I would sit there for what seemed like hours, hiding amongst the leaves and the Granny Smiths, communing with nature and my innermost thoughts.

DIARY ENTRY
FRIDAY 18th MARCH, 2005 – HEATHROW

Well the day has finally arrived. The friend who drops us off at the airport remarks that with my hair in pigtails I look like a 10-year-old, which is actually how I feel. Although so much of my life has already passed, it feels as if my whole life is in front of me. The check-in girl tells us she had a friend who went to New Zealand, and is now living there with a wife and family. This comment wiggles its way into my brain, and jiggles around with my discontent, and I lose myself in imaginings and writing as my daughter spends a very happy 20 minutes in Duty Free.

DIARY ENTRY
19th/20th MARCH, 2005 – SYDNEY

The flight into Sydney is spectacular, and we land at 8.30 a.m. after an exhausting journey via LA. Taxi to hotel is easy, if expensive, but the hotel is fine and on budget; it has hot water and what feels like comfortable beds. I cannot wait to spend a good night's sleep on a bed. We check in early, and after a coffee and a bath, make our way to Darling Harbour, which is busy with Sunday punters.

We have a pleasant lunch followed by an ice cream. A trip on the monorail, takes us to the hotel and abortive calls to my daughter in New Zealand. It is really hard trying to keep awake, and we grab an hour's sleep before we hit the Hard Rock Cafe.

The Hard Rock Cafe is a taste of familiarity in an unknown city. It reminds me of the Mondrian painting in the Tate, holding us safely in the known. A comforting benefit of globalisation. We walk through the streets of old terraced houses with balconies, which vastly contrast the Sydney Skyline. They are delightful. It is barely 5 p.m., and we need to stay awake for at least another four hours. It feels like an impossible task. A trip to the Sky Tower should do the trick. We wander back past the Cathedral and the Anzac memorial, and buy our tickets for the rollercoaster ride into the clouds. It does nothing for our jet lag, but the view is magnificent and worth every penny. The lights are coming on across the city and we are treated to a breathtaking sunset. We hit the sack after navigating the giant bats in Hyde Park. I sleep until 5.30 p.m. and then dose until 7.30 p.m. We have cracked it. Ready for a new day.

DIARY ENTRY
MONDAY 21st MARCH, 2005 – SYDNEY

Breakfast, emails, then through the Botanical Gardens to the Opera House. In the gardens we find the colony of bats hanging upside down by the cafe. They are huge and very noisy, and really rather daunting, but like most things, less daunting in the light of day. The trees are absolutely amazing, especially the enormous *fig tree. I am reminded of our business logo; an acorn running off to be a tree. I imagine a baby fig with arms, legs, and a very fetching hat doing the same thing. Trees are very good at just being what they are.*

The Sydney Opera House is like a vision. I have seen the image so many times, but it still feels as if I am in a dream. Its beautiful white peaks travel upwards, creating a beautiful silhouette against the bright blue sky. The architect Jorn Utzon, was initially rejected by three judges in a 1956 competition to design the building, but his entry was picked out by the fourth judge, renowned American architect Eero Saarinen, who declared it outstanding. Mr Utzon beat 232 other entrants and won £5,000 for his design. Apparently during the 1980s, a net was put in place above the orchestra pit in the Opera Theatre, after a live chicken walked off the stage during a performance of Boris Godunov and landed on a cellist. I rest my case. Find a space and stay centre stage.

Of course family and friends will often reject our ideas about ourselves, sowing seeds of doubt, and this moves us away from the light at our centre, pushing and pulling us back into the wings. But external references do not make dreams come true, internal references do. Once you feel secure in your plan or idea, referring to those who can help you achieve your goal can be helpful, but at the end of the day your guts are your best judge.

I had learnt about visualisation during the Tony Robbins experience in my 4 year, and had been working on trying to manifest what was in my heart, although it seemed to be taking some time to work out exactly what that was. The idea is to project yourself to where you are trying to get to. The big picture. See yourself standing in that place of greatest achievement. How do you look, how do you feel, what can you see around you? In order to manifest something you need to visualise in detail, to enhance the image; vision; sound; feel. Once you have your vision, and this can take some time, you can make it more colourful, turn up the sound or increase the feelings around the vision and this will secure it firmly in your mind's eye.

I look to the Opera House and contemplate the fact that this was once someone's vision, and there it stands larger than life, inviting us into the sanctuary within. Surely everything starts out as a vision in our heads. You are told when visualising not to worry about the whys and wherefores of reaching your goal, as the 'Universe' will take care of everything. Just hold the vision and allow things to fall into place. Easier said than done, and for now I am clutching my vision tightly to my chest, just in case I lose it in the sea, drop it on the floor, or carelessly decide to toss it aside.

Tosca, our opera of choice is packed. It is wonderful – a faultless production in a magnificent setting. A well spent £140.00 per ticket, in spite of the fact that my daughter, who is still suffering from the effects of jet lag sleeps through everything, apart of course from the interval ice cream! It is an experience she will never forget. We walk back in the rain via the all night Quickie Mart, and buy a variety of rubbish food fit for a midnight feast! There are only two of us, but it feels like a 'Famous Five' adventure. We eat, drink, and fall asleep, tired but happy.

DIARY ENTRY
TUESDAY 22nd MARCH, 2005 – SYDNEY

It is the evening before I leave for New Zealand, in search of a new direction. As I drift into unconsciousness I am awoken by the need to urinate. As I try to return to my repose I place my hand on my body and hope that my attempt at 'self' Reiki practice will help me.

Reiki is a Japanese technique for stress reduction and relaxation, that also promotes healing. It is administered by 'laying on hands' and is based on the idea that an unseen 'life force energy' flows through us and is what causes us to be alive. If one's 'life force energy' is low, then we are more likely to get sick or feel stress, and if it is high, we are more capable of being happy and healthy. The word Reiki is made of two Japanese words – Rei which means 'God's wisdom or the higher power' and Ki which is 'life force energy'. So Reiki is actually 'spiritually guided life force energy.'

I had recently taken a Reiki course and was keen to increase my knowledge, and also to see if I could use it to induce sleep.

It has the opposite effect. I feel my hands tingle violently as an energy runs through my body; an energy which has been absent in the recent months. Two years ago in Malta, I had hit upon the idea that part of my destiny was to write. I doubted and gave way to other ideas, but now the idea is back. I must gather my thoughts and put pen to paper. In my imaginings New Zealand is significant and so is Fiji. I don't yet know why, but if I listen carefully, maybe I will find out. A storm is brewing outside shaking the windows, and whistling through the rafters and vents, as a new energy courses through my body. I close my eyes and try to sleep.

DIARY ENTRY
WEDNESDAY 23rd MARCH, 2005 – SYDNEY

I have been awake all night with anticipation and ideas. Today we leave for New Zealand. We make it to the airport in plenty of time, ready for a delay. The flight passes without incident, and we arrive in Wellington, having flown across the most awesome sight I have ever seen. After queuing to get through customs and immigration, we grab a taxi, and make for Bas BackPackers. Oh my goodness, the view from the top floor room is absolutely amazing. There are windows all around the room, and we look down on the harbour, and the cinema, where the premier of 'Lord of the Rings' was shown. It is like something out of the 1950s. In fact its older as it is Art Deco, and so is the rest of the place; it's like stepping back 50 years. I love it. We visit the museum, and then have hot chocolate and cake in the cinema foyer. Excellent.

DIARY ENTRY
THURSDAY 25th MARCH, 2005 – NEW ZEALAND

Today we travel to South Island on the InterIslander Ferry. I have been looking forward to this part of the adventure, and I am not disappointed. It is magnificent and takes my breath away. The sun is shining, despite the forecast and we spend a happy three hours looking at the scenery, reading and soaking up the sun. We collect our car and make our way to Abel Tasman National Park. When we arrive at the chalets in Marahau, having traversed mountains, plains, and quaint villages, it is raining hard. We are shown to our chalet, and are completely knocked out by the view. We walk to the local shop, getting soaked in the process. We check out the restaurant and book a table for later. We return, eat to our hearts content, and go to bed tired, full, and exceedingly happy.

DIARY ENTRY
FRIDAY 25th MARCH, 2005 (GOOD FRIDAY) – NEW ZEALAND

We dodge the rain, and have breakfast up at the cafe attached to the office, and then book horse riding and kayaking trips.

The guy running the horse riding, Brian, is off the planet. His eyes are amazing, and I can't seem to avert my gaze. The rain is intermittent, but we book it anyway. We walk along the beach and paddle in the Tasman Sea, and then have lunch. We make it back to the car just before we get drenched again. After a rest we head back for horse riding. Brian is very emotional and skitty. I somehow manage to ascertain that he is a Cancerian – and there is a full moon! Well that explains it. Cancerians are ruled by the moon making them very susceptible to its energy, especially when it is full. We feel as if we will never leave as he fusses around the horses and the equipment, back and forth and back and forth again, looking like a rabbit trying to avoid the headlights. But we eventually leave. The ride across the beach is spectacular. Rain, sun, wind, rain, sun, wind. It is worth the wait. Now as I sit painting the view, which changes every second, making it rather difficult to capture, I feel my muscles starting to complain. We are looking forward to dinner at the same restaurant as last night. Tonight we will continue working our way through the pudding menu – tomorrow kayaking with the seals.

On our way to the restaurant we see a night rainbow. Wow... Judy Garland springs to the forefront of my mind, complete with bluebirds, and the notion that dreams really do come true. The moons rays are beyond beauty. It is like a spotlight on a vast watery stage, inviting you to step into the centre. I make a wish. We channel our inner Judy's and sing our way to the restaurant. This sight stays in my mind, and an idea for a Personal Philosophy Programme starts to take form.

I discover after my trip, in a magazine sent to me by a friend, that New Zealand is famous for rainbows; in fact the author of the article Peter Walker refers to it as the Rainbow Nation. He also talks of the scepticism that should be levelled at anyone telling you they have seen a night rainbow; 'it is a rare and almost mythical thing', and goes on to write of his experience. *'And yet there in the dark New Zealand sky, just before midnight, was an arch of light hanging between the hills of a valley fifty miles from Auckland. Physics is physics: the New Zealand sky, with its extraordinary clarity and moisture-laden winds, is the natural home of rainbows, and there is no reason why this principle should cease at nightfall.'* He speaks of the sheer brilliance of the moonlight forming the milky bow, which he sees in the Coromandel Hills, a few miles inland from Hauraki Gulf, where the world's yachting billionaires gather to duel for the America's Cup. I wonder if he too made a wish.

DIARY ENTRY
SUNDAY 27th MARCH, 2005 (EASTER SUNDAY) – NEW ZEALAND

I meditate and see a circle of children. I am sitting with them under a very bright light. I don't know where the light is, but I think it is here. I also see adults standing around the edge of the circle, and have an overwhelming feeling of love.

We leave Marahau, and make our way back to the ferry terminal. We take the 'scenic route' which is stunning, taking us down through the Marlborough Sounds to Picton. We find it hilarious that we have seen a sign saying 'Scenic Route', as everything we have seen so far has been exactly that. My daughter buys me a beautiful necklace and I am very touched by it. I don't understand it's meaning until many years later, but it is The Koru (Ma̅ori for 'loop'). It is a spiral shape based on the appearance of a new unfurling silver fern frond. It is an integral symbol in Ma¯ori art, carving, and tattooing, where it symbolises new life, growth, strength, and peace. It's shape conveys the idea of perpetual movement, while the inner coil suggests returning to the point of origin. Her thoughtfulness warms my heart. It's symbolism enchants me, and seems to echo the journey that I am on, the journey back to the centre.

There are many other discoveries to make before we cross back over to North Island. We visit some of the most beautiful and curious places on earth, and are completely lost in our travels. We marvel at waterfalls, and are mesmerised by glow worm caves, vast tracts of open spaces, and towering mountains. Nothing is booked, and we go completely with the flow, enhancing our sense of adventure. But it is time to head for Auckland and the main reason for our visit. Catching up with my eldest daughter.

DIARY ENTRY
MONDAY 30th MARCH, 2005 – NEW ZEALAND

We leave Wellington and sit on the train for hours. We eventually pull into Auckland around 10 p.m. and make our way to the hostel. My daughter and her travelling companion are standing outside waiting for us. After much outpouring of emotion, we find our room and spend an hour catching up and handing over mail. In the morning we make our way to the harbour for breakfast and bask in the sun. We take a trip to the sky tower, and I spend the afternoon reading a new book 'A Land of Two Halves' by Joe Bennett. The irony is not lost on me as I contemplate my own duality.

DIARY ENTRY
TUESDAY 31st MARCH, 2005 – NEW ZEALAND

We take the ferry to Waiheke Island where my nephew and his wife live. My eldest daughter is already starting to get irritated with me, so it's just as well she is going to Fiji early. I guess I am in full 'mummy mode', and have completely forgotten that she has been travelling, quite happily for several months without me wittering in her ear, making suggestions that she doesn't need, and asking her if she has drunk enough water, and put her sun cream on; once a mummy, always a mummy! My nephew meets us at the ferry terminal, and we make our way to the house. We love it. I am hooked. In fact I was from the minute I stepped onto the ferry, which gave me such a feeling of freedom. We visit the beach and have lunch. Perfection. The afternoon is spent talking, chilling, and looking at old photos. There is a picture of our family home in Camberley in amongst them, the home we had recently all been wrenched from. My daughter remarks that her life was 'perfect there'. To me it feels like another life – it certainly wasn't perfect for me. But then everyone's perfect is so very different.

DIARY ENTRY
WEDNESDAY 1st APRIL, 2005 – NEW ZEALAND

My daughter and I fall out. She has asked me to take something back to England for her. She presents me with a large bag full of leaflets, which she has collected on her travels. It is extremely heavy, and I question her need for them, and point out that I am trying to 'travel light'. This doesn't go down very well, and she clearly wants to pass the burden onto me.

The feisty 1 vibrational force is running riot on the day in question. It is the 1st of April, which is the month of Aries, and the Aries fiery energy is connected to the number 1. My birthday is the 1st June, and her Destiny number is a number 1… that's a lot of 1s all coming together on the same day and they are all centred in self. Stood under the spotlight of the 1 energy, you will encounter everything needed to be a pioneer and leader; dynamism, independence, boldness, creativity, etc, however you may also encounter arrogance, rigidity, selfishness, stubbornness, and an extremely headstrong will. But this usually rears up when your back is against the wall, or fear is lurking in the wings.

I leave the car keys and make for the beach. Good decision. I meet some of the locals; Diedre, Jim, and Ronnie the plasterer. The girls eventually turn up and buy me a coffee, hugs become the order of the day and are offered, along with forgiveness, which is given and received. Diedre and Jim are delightful, and we chat about the ins and outs of living on the island. I go to Jim and Diedre's later in the day to get the number for Cindy who has recently moved to Waiheke. When I call she invites me over for tea, and I hear all about how hard it is to move to New Zealand. Hard, but obviously possible. I feel an excitement I haven't felt for a very long time, and think about what it would take to get myself here. I would certainly need the props of a pioneer; a cloak of courage, my pioneering pants, a sword of strong will, and probably some sandwiches!

The island has completely captured my heart. I feel totally at one with the vibe here. Over the next few days we are taken to outdoor markets, where people mingle happily, embracing the community spirit which is palpable. We visit the most beautiful beaches, and swim in the refreshing waters.

My body feels relaxed, and I can see that my daughters clearly love it here. I feel connected to everything, and yet love the feeling of separation brought about by island living. This would appear to suit me well. A seed is planted, and I leave it on a very different beach to the one in Hartlepool.

As the ferry heads back towards Auckland, after our few days spent with family, my eyes well with tears. I am faced with something I really didn't want to get rid of or leave behind.

DIARY ENTRY
WEDNESDAY 6th APRIL, 2005 – NEW ZEALAND

My daughter navigates brilliantly to the airport Rent a Dent office, and we get there in plenty of time, with no new dents. My heart is heavy when we take off, as I see Auckland and Waiheke in the distance. I wonder if we will ever return, as I soar into the blue, and onto another adventure.

DIARY ENTRY
THURSDAY 7th APRIL, 2005 – FIJI

We head for Fiji. We had wanted to stay in New Zealand longer, but unfortunately we didn't know this when the arrangements were made so we go with the flow. The temperature when we arrive in Nandi is stifling. My daughter and her travelling companion had gone on ahead, and they meet us at the airport. They had been at the Nandi Bay Resort for three days already and are loving it. But it's not for me, due to the student vibe, and not so comfortable accommodation. We transfer to a small island the next morning, and take up residence in a small village of well-appointed huts, complete with swimming pool. I am emotional when I leave my daughter, as I won't see her for another month. I have told her of my desire to move to New Zealand and she is very unhappy about it.

The heat hits us, and makes me feel quite low. I feel like the two-toed sloth in 'Life of Pi', and feel like sleeping for most of the day. I ask Sophie 'what is the best way to live' like this, at a snail's pace, or at the frenetic pace of the UK. She says New Zealand is the way to live. I agree. So what about Europe, what about Edinburgh, what about friends, family, commitments, what about James, what about Michelle? What about the business? What are my duties and responsibilities?

Tomorrow there is an eclipse and a new moon, and with it I hope some clarity, some:

· new ideas
· new opportunities
· new people
· new places
· new love

or will there just be a realisation that what I already have is enough.

That night I continue to read *Life of Pi*, a book exchanged in the office in Nandi for *An Island of Two Halves*. The Universe presents me with more questions needing answers.

Why do people move? What makes them uproot and leave everything they've known for a great unknown beyond the horizon? Why climb this Mount Everest of formalities that makes you feel like a beggar? Why enter this jungle of foreignness where everything is new, strange, and difficult? The answer is the same the world over: people move in the hope of a better life.

DIARY ENTRY
FRIDAY 8th APRIL, 2005 – FIJI

Well the day has arrived, the day of the eclipse. I had anticipated this day with trepidation thinking it to be an omen in my life; but life goes on as usual. The ants carry on marching, the birds carry on singing, the tide has just gone out and will shortly come in again. So what has changed for me? I am a little bit older, a little less rich, my hair has grown, I have experienced the beauty of New Zealand, been to the Sydney Opera House, and unsettled my daughters.

I have not met my soulmate, fallen in love, or won the lottery.

It is 1.30 a.m. and we have been hit by torrential rain. No sign of an eclipse, but the sky is very dark. Sitting under the protection of the covered terrace, with a strong breeze blowing in along with the odd drop of rain, is very refreshing; the humidity here is so high here. Maybe this is a clearing out process before the arrival of the new moon.

I make a list of what I want gone from my life:

· Negative thinking
· Fear
· Unfit body
· Disempowering friends
· Disempowering neighbours

· *Unfocused thinking*
· *Overspending on irrelevant things*
· *Waste: wasted thoughts, ideas, food.*

I must be relentless: like this rain; otherwise what will I achieve?

Will I ever have a house by the sea, where I can listen to the waves rolling in, whilst I think, create, meditate, write my book, develop a course, entertain, earn enough money to travel, see my family?

Today we bury the Pope. Tomorrow Charles gets married.

The storm has passed – it is much cooler. Sophie and I take a Kayak around the jetty.

There has been no eclipse – no darkness – no returning light. I am confused – did I get it wrong? I feel a weight of disappointment after so much expectation.

As I take a nap I try some Reiki. Once again my hands get hot and tingly, especially around my heart and abdomen chakras. I feel uneasy here and long to be back in New Zealand.

DIARY ENTRY
SATURDAY 9th APRIL, 2005 – FIJI

There is nothing to do here – except nothing.

I know now that I am not one for tropical islands; especially ones with creepy crawlies and things that sting you in taxis. The people however, are beautiful. I drink Cava, the local knock you out, and I am duly knocked out.

I come up with a plan. Sell flat – rent somewhere and buy a place in Waiheke. Wait until Sophie has finished her GCSEs then move there. I ponder on what would truly make my life better. An answer I am not expecting pops into my head. A soulmate.

DIARY ENTRY
15ᵗʰ APRIL, 2005 – ASCOT

Well it feels ok to be home. Didn't think it would, but it does.

My business partner has asked the question 'are you going back?' The answer is yes – but not for two years until after Sophie's GCSEs; well that's the plan. I can always change my mind. I have a lot of research to do, and costings.

My astrology for 15th April, 2005 says:

'Your world is changing, both internally and externally. You feel a need to broaden your horizons. You contemplate a move to a new neighbourhood or a trip to a faraway land. The people in your life will change as a result of this. You are about to embark on a new phase in your life and these new friends will act as guides.'

I clutch at my necklace and take a deep breath. New Zealand has opened my heart and my head, and I desperately want to be there.

On my return to England I tried to sell my flat, but it was impossible. Any interest immediately fell by the wayside due to the short lease and difficulty with the neighbours, which was growing worse each day, and was in desperate need of resolution. Until I had renewed the lease no-one was going to buy it. This was an ongoing drama with many players, and the stage was feeling very crowded, and so I decided to retreat backstage, and deal with it from a distance. To this end I rent out my flat, and move to the village where my daughters' school, and my business is based. I was not only going to have freedom from the double school run, and the chaos of Burleigh Wood House, but I would be receiving more from my rental than I would be paying out. What was not to like? I was hoping that it would enable me to deal with the ins and outs of the lease renewal, without the burden of the emotional upset that seemed to creep in every time I pulled into the drive.

There were four flats in total. The neighbours above me had been in dispute with their neighbour on the other side of the fence, long before I had arrived. Unfortunately, I had arrived in the middle of the dispute, and had found myself immediately harangued by both sides. My beautiful flat, which had now been completely renovated, including a new bathroom courtesy of the piano funds, belied the awfulness and strangeness of what was going on.

As flat owners we were all entitled to one vote per flat. I had mine, my upstairs neighbour had hers, but our neighbour on the other side had control of three votes. His own, the proxy vote he held for the absent woman in the upstairs flat, and his casting vote as chairman.

This made it impossible to move anything forward especially, given the level of hostility created, before my time, which festered like an open wound. He had all the power. As things unfolded, I became aware that he'd had control for years.

The feeling of relief at moving out was immense. I left all of my furniture there, and luckily had enough money to furnish the new flat. This suited me, my seven 5s and the added vibration of the 5 year very well. I mostly love change, and spent a happy time buying new things for the flat, and generally felt as if I had moved on with my life. Of course the problem needed resolution, but the changes were much welcomed. Real freedom from the situation was clearly going to take a lot of discipline and more time. In the meantime I decide to concentrate on exercise, change my diet and meditate more. My daughter was starting her GCSEs, and had the freedom to walk to school and become more independent. The flat was small but had everything we needed, along with the added benefit of being above a cafe which I loved.

Before I had made the move, my philosophical journey had continued, and had taken me down a route where I had concluded that the flat was not my home; it was just an asset. It was the accumulation of my financial past. It did not represent anything which made me feel secure. In fact I had spent a lot of time feeling increasingly insecure, and with a feeling that I would never escape it's clutches. I had moved there to accommodate the piano, something which had seemed so important. But what had that got to do with security. It was gone. Things go, we cannot hold on to anything.

I had decided, that for me, security is found within being – it is internal – not external.

Bricks and mortar are just a casing. Maybe I needed another way to live? I continued to question the whole idea of security. Was it something that would make me feel grounded, or was it something that would hold me back?

What makes me feel safe/secure?

Partner	*No*
House	*No*
Friends	*No*
Family	*Yes/No/Don't know?*
What I do	*Yes*

What I stand for   Yes
Who I am   Yes
Being on the right path Yes

This had all been contemplated during a sojourn to Wiltshire. The house that I was staying in belonged to some dear friends, and held me lovingly in its architectural arms. It's calming colours and beautiful views, soothed my soul whilst I pondered my current position.

DIARY ENTRY

MAY HALF TERM, 2005 – WILTSHIRE

The stream below the house is a work of art which is constantly moving, as it flows rapidly along its course. The water moves the reeds, and small pebbles, constantly changing the patterns. I am drawn inexplicably to this fast-moving, ever-changing environment. It holds me in its power, and I feel at one with it. My nature is to change, to explore, to reveal the new and the exciting, in a search for the truth. I feel as if I am slowly turning towards my centre. As I look at the stream I wonder at its ability to flow so effortlessly and I charge myself with using the energy of this 5 year to do the same.

At FASBAT we have been working on a show with the Senior girls. The title of the show is 'The Dating Game'. We play around with an Adrian Mole sketch, our version of a TV dating game, and generally explore the theme of love. There is a lot of giggling as the girls explore unrequited love, unconditional love, and the thrills and spills of first love. We have a lot of fun, and the girls get the opportunity to delve into one of life's most interesting challenges through drama.

Strangely I fall into a relationship at exactly the same time as I move to my new surroundings, just before the performance, and once again the synchronicity of my work/life themes astound me. Looking back I can see that in spite of the pain I had been through, the idea of relationship was never far away; after all I had perhaps foolishly persuaded myself that I would meet a soulmate on the other side of the world. In a year when sexual energy is, according to most writers around the subject of numerology extremely high, I guess if it was going to happen, this could be seen as perfect timing. In my heart I guess relationships felt like one of my biggest failures, and I was always searching to turn it to success. Gemini is the sign of the Twins, and in spite of my hermit-like 7 destiny number, I always seem to be looking for my lost twin.

The American writer Richard Bach says that:

'A soulmate is someone who has locks that fit our keys, and keys to fit our locks. When we feel safe enough to open the locks, our truest selves step out, and we can be completely and honestly who we are'.

I had resolved to take flight and disappear to New Zealand, but what now? As the relationship developed I was challenged on many levels. Far more difficult to go with the flow, when the person you are with is travelling up through their own massive personal development curve. But having read that we learn the most about ourselves through relationship, I braved the storm.

I find myself for the most part happy with this excursion into the unknown, although terrified at the same time. I may have four new walls about me and a shiny new roof, but the elephant had somehow managed to squeeze through an open window, and take up residence in the lounge; quite an effort given that the flat is on the first floor! It is once again the date of my mother's birthday, 16th August. I receive a phone call saying that my new partner wants to call the whole thing off. The abandonment issue relating to my mother hits me full in the face. It is August, my 4 month in my 5 year and it feels as if any foundations I have managed to build have been shaken back down to the ground.

DIARY ENTRY

AUGUST, 2005 – ASCOT

Right, so you just can't have the ecstasy without the agony. I have been in agony all day, in contrast to the ecstasy experienced last week.

As I mentioned earlier the 5 energy can take you from good to bad, bad to good, and then back again, such is its mercurial nature. Expect the unexpected. My emotions are left close to the edge of my existence, and my diary shows me going through a labyrinth of opposite emotions and asking myself the following question:

Is it better to feel something, rather than nothing? I have two options:
Retreat or face the fear…

The fear is bigger than any wave, and I need to use all my resources to keep it down on the beach. I didn't set the pace, he did and now he is retreating. Go with the flow, go with the flow.

We all need to know what our fear looks like in order to keep it in check. I had luckily been through a visualisation process to identify mine, at the fire-walk seminar. It takes the form of a very large wave. I had learnt to lessen it's effect by visualising the wave, and reducing it to a trickle. When you know what something looks like you can deal with it a lot better. Once I have the physical feeling of fear under control, I ask myself some sensible questions.

What am I frightened of? The answers are clear and I am sure universal:
· *Rejection*
· *Loss*
· *Mis-interpretation*
· *Pain*
· *Loneliness*

This week I have been on rollercoaster of emotion. I have felt:

Alive	*Powerless*
Serene	*Anxious*
Balanced	*Scared*
Peaceful	*Uncomfortable*
Confident	*Uncertain*
Joyful	*Vulnerable*
Sensual	*Drained*
Fulfilled	*Overwhelmed*
Alert	*Deflated*
Sensitive	*Confused*
Free	*Lost*

We find that we are just as scared as each other, and after a lot of talking, we manage to face the fear together and agree to carry on at a much slower pace.

I have a trip planned to the Edinburgh Fringe; an annual pilgrimage taken each August with a Scottish girlfriend. We have been friends since we met on the path to the Swimming Pool Lecture Hall, during our late entry to university life at Royal

Holloway, our joint fear of academia forming a strong bond. The trip comes at the perfect time, and we spend a week in each others company along with two other friends from Ascot. We take to the stage acting out the part of free spirits; laughing, taking our chance on shows, and generally having a great time.

DIARY ENTRY
THURSDAY 24th AUGUST, 2005 – EDINBURGH

Sitting here in the late summer sun, on the park bench gifted by Vivian McKendick's husband, because 'she loved Edinburgh', I feel totally serene. The cacophony of sounds does not dissipate my mood – the pan pipes, the bag pipes, the train, the traffic, the voices, the brass band.

I am reminded of my trip to the South Bank at the beginning of the year, and once more I am feeling connected to everything. I return to Ascot refreshed and keen to navigate the rest of the 5 year journey. It is a rollercoaster, but I am happy to flow with the changing circumstances which have taken me closer to myself and what I want. I have selfishly put most things aside in order to heal myself with the help of another. I have stood at the crossroads, which often appear in a 5 year, and faced it with a greater knowledge of myself and what I have to offer a relationship. I have resolved with myself not to compromise, but to stick closely to things which empower me, moving away from situations and people who do not. You would think that this is an easy thing to do. Easy – no. Possible – yes.

I could have chosen to avoid pain by not entering into a relationship, but I chose the other path and faced my fear. Christmas sees my family elsewhere. I see them briefly for present swapping and hugs, and then turn my attention towards

Christmas, in a year which has been mostly about myself and my inner journey.

December in a 5 year equates to an 8 month. One of the themes of the number 8 is Power and Authority, and as I meander backwards through my journey, I imagine myself standing in the centre of the light thrown down by the moon onto the sea in Marahau. I have travelled over a vast distance this year, physically, mentally, and emotionally, and I am standing in a much stronger place. Although there are many issues still unresolved concerning my dealings at Burleigh Wood House, my business, and my new partnership, I am feeling blessed and confident that my power and authority are starting to look a little different. The promise that the 5 holds for freedom, progress, and change resounds loud and clear, filling my life with a new understanding that progress is always at the end of difficulty. Clearly a good thing to remember, as I leave the year behind me.

YEAR 6:

THE NURTURER

Keywords: Support · Service · Harmony · Balance

Underbalanced	**Right Action**	**Overbalanced**
martyr		*argumentative*
nasty		*worried*
selfish	DUTIFUL	*possesive*
tactless	HELPFUL	*negative*
intolerant	FRIENDLY	*critical*
uncooperative	TOLERANT	*interfering*
	SUPPORTIVE	
	DEPENDABLE	

BALANCE DUTY WITH CREATIVE EXPRESSION

CHARACTER BRIEF
Loving individual looking to serve

Costume	Props
Duffle Coat of Duty	Romantic Novel
Robe of Responsibility	Tin of Chicken Soup
Hairband of Harmony	Nugget of Nurture

■ 666666666(33)666666666 ■

YEAR 6:

NO PLACE LIKE HOME

A 6 Personal Year is a year of creative development, and a wonderful year for forming meaningful, lasting relationships. It is often a year when deep friendships are cemented into marriage. Harmony is important and one naturally feels a sense of duty to family and community during this cycle. The lesson is to find balance between expression and creative energy (which is important for your inner-harmony) and the time given to family affairs. It is a very conducive vibration to develop our creative faculties.

Joanne Warmsley
Sacred Scribes

A list made at the front end of my 6 Personal Year, alerts me to the many duties and responsibilities that stand before me. There was dissonance everywhere and I was given plenty of opportunity to balance and harmonise.

Burleigh Wood House matters
Family matters
Relationship matters
Business matters
Me matters

The number 6 is linked to the astrological sign of Cancer, the earth mother. Love is at its core, and I like to think of the number as a pregnant woman, closeting her child in a warm and safe embrace whilst it grows and develops, ready to take its place in the world.

As I have matured and moved from epicycle to epicycle, the idea of harmony, beauty, and service has grown within me forming a central core. The desire to do good in the world is the driving force, and although I have been in situations where I have not been able to manifest this directly, with hindsight, I can see clearly how I have returned to it time and time again. The phrase 'you've made a real difference' is one that makes my heart sing, and is top of my list of core values. I love to be around people who are bent on making a difference in this world, and when I am with them, they feel like family. Using my creative energy to beautify my surroundings is something I have a flair for, and the look and feel of my home is very important to me. This is probably why I never balk at the prospect of moving, as it is such a great opportunity to engage in the process of beautification.

Sometimes I have done this with the benefit of a large budget, and sometimes on a shoestring. Whatever the circumstance I always find the process rewarding. When the last coat of paint is on the wall, the cushions are lined up on the sofa, and my world is tidy, I feel a satisfying sense of harmony. It is then, and only then, that I can start to create and build.

My first experience of musical harmony was singing in the school choir. Simple music at first and then more complex. My Music Teacher Mr Piercy was my hero at school, and I was keen to do well in this subject. I clearly had an aptitude for it, as my reports show A for effort, and A for ability. It is here that I learnt about harmony and dissonance. When dissonance is found in music, the sweetness of the harmonic experience disappears, and is replaced by a harsh sound. The same dissonance happens for me when the colour isn't quite right, and the cushions are all over the place. Some people simply can't stand any form of musical dissonance, it gives them the same feeling as fingernails scratching a blackboard, but I revel in the opportunity to restore the music back to a harmonic sound, composer being willing.

According to legend, Pythagoras discovered the foundations of musical tuning by listening to the sounds of the blacksmith's hammers, which produced consonance and dissonance when they were struck simultaneously. He used ratios to work out the musical scale and the principles that govern music, apply to the vibratory rate of colours, and the same ratio exists between colours of the spectrum and between notes of the musical scale.

One of the fondest memories of my childhood home and family harmony, is pretending to be a Tiller Girl on a Sunday night, whilst watching Sunday Night at the London Palladium with my parents. There wasn't much room behind the sofa, but it was just enough for a temporary stage. My parents loved the programme, the music, dancing, and the variety of acts presented, and seemed to enjoy me prancing around attempting to do high kicks; there was much laughter. The day had typically started with Sunday School, followed by the Sunday lunch ritual. Roast beef, Yorkshire puddings, and all the trimmings. In the afternoon we would take a trip in the much loved family car, or walk around the neighbourhood. Sunday always felt harmonious; maybe because it vibrates to the number 7, my Life Path Number, and the number connected to spirituality and mysticism. The shops were still closed on a Sunday giving the day a very different feel, the feel of a sabbatical. To my mind the loss of this 'day of rest' has had a detrimental effect on society.

The number 7 is often described as the hermit. It has an air of being in the world, but not of the world; and this is often how I felt, always happiest in my own little world. In the film *Schindler's List* there is a sequence featuring a little girl dressed in red, one of only a few instances of colour in a black and white film. She is walking through a scene of devastation. The film is about The Holocaust, and the significance of her role in the film is far removed from my world; however, when I saw the image for the first time it touched me deeply, and I identified with it 100 per cent. Sometimes when I am feeling the 7 vibration very strongly, it can feel as if the whole world is moving around me in slow motion. It is a strange feeling, but one I rather like. To me it is a harmonious state, although anyone encountering me in it, may find the energy aloof, detached, unresponsive, and otherwise engaged in thought.

Much of my free time as a child was spent at the top of the much loved apple tree, gazing out at the field at the back of the house, or in the shed teaching myself to play the piano from an old Methodist hymn book. My brothers, who were a lot older than me, had left home, leaving me with a rather singular childhood. There was a definite tension between the early experience of my number 6 Life Cycle number, and my number 7 Life Path Number, giving me my first taste of 'conscious' dissonance, as opposed to musical dissonance.

There are three Life Path Cycles which are calculated from your date of birth, and these are very revealing when looking backwards into childhood memories.

The number representing the month of birth, reduced to a single digit or master number, is the first Life Path period indicator. The second Life Path period is determined by the day of birth, reduced to a single digit or master number. The final Life Path period is based on the year of birth reduced to a single digit or master number.

My First Life Path Cycle was a 6, as I was born in June, and this sat next to my 7 Life Path Number, which is in operation from birth to death. Looking back I can clearly see how these two numbers created an uncomfortable and confusing experience in my early years.

My bothers had both gone, and although my parents provided a family home, and everything I needed in terms of practical care, I felt estranged, and generally struggled, except of course on a Sunday when the dissonance seemed to resolve. Although I didn't realise it at the time, I was resonating strongly with the 6 energy which is the number concerned with harmony, beauty and service. I was learning harmony through music, and this was my main interest. I remember begging my parents to let me decorate my room, and paint the brown furniture white, which after a lot of persuasion they allowed, giving me the opportunity to beautify my surroundings, and I clearly remember thinking, on our Sunday afternoon walk around the neighbourhood, how much I would like to sort out the dishevelled and unloved gardens, or paint the front door a different colour. I loved being in the garden, and reports from school show my interest in music, embroidery, and art, at the forefront of my achievements. I am described as friendly and helpful, and I clearly had a desire to serve, although my mathematics grades were decidedly disappointing!

But the 7 energy dragged me away into my mysterious world, time and time again, and I must have seemed like a very strange child, as I sat in the shed for hours trying to work out the notes in front of me on the piano, or hidden away in my newly decorated cave trying to order my possessions. The shed of course had to have curtains and pictures on its walls, which I managed to achieve by rescuing things on the way out... I'm sure the spiders were very appreciative!

I now view my early years and the dissonance contained within it as an initiation in the central theme of Pythagorean thought.

The modern usage of number is as a sign, to denote a specific quantity or amount, but for the Pythagoreans number was not something to be used, rather, its nature is to be discovered. This I was clearly not going to learn in a maths class, but through a lifelong search for the truth. The rub was real, and now makes sense.

One of the most helpful things about numerology, is its ability to help you understand other people. How often have you met someone and felt a sense of dissonance, a feeling of being 'out of tune' with something, or someone? The harmony just isn't there. Having done many charts for people, I have encountered the difficulty when two numbers, an odd number, and an even number, sit side by side. This can cause confusion within the person's chart, and can also cause dis-harmony within a relationship, unless there is some understanding of the energies at play.

It is clear to see that if you are in a 7 Personal Year, and are feeling the need to be on your own, to contemplate your navel, and take yourself on a journey of inner learning and discovery, and your partner is in a 6 Personal Year, and wants to be helpful, wants to share, and feel needed, then this will present a difficulty. It is hard to feel needed when your partner wants to be alone. If you are in a 5 year and your partner is in a 4, then your need to be free flowing and adventurous, may clash with the serious hard-working vibration of your partner's 4 year. As human beings we are very good at taking things personally, and the behaviour of another human being can sow seeds of doubt, giving rise to anxieties and fear. Once we step out of our balanced centre, and into our overbalanced or underbalanced energy, we may as well leave the stage.

In this above scenario, the 6 may well turn, through fear, to become intolerant, possessive, and critical, and the 7 in response may become distant, detached, impatient, and unresponsive. You can see the difficulty. Of course, with work and enlightenment these differences can be ironed out, and understood, although at times, it is hard to explain to another person exactly what you are feeling. In the book *The Four Agreements* by the Mexican writer, teacher, and Shaman Miguel Ruiz, he suggests that we take nothing personally. '*Whatever happens around you, don't take it personally. Nothing other people do is because of you. It is because of themselves. All people live in their own dream, in their own mind; they are in a completely different world from the one we live in. When we take something personally, we make the assumption that they know what is in our world, and we try to impose our world on their world.*'

If we can come to understand ourselves better, and the energies at work throughout the numerological cycles, then we can better communicate our world to others and bring about harmony, or at least dissipate the dissonance. Of course the ideal would be to just to accept everyone as they are, and for them to accept us, just the way we are, to love unconditionally. But this would appear to be a long way down the spiritual road. Until we love ourselves unconditionally, there is no hope for anyone else.

If you have ever played squash you will know that the centre of the court is where it's at. There is a T junction in the middle of the court, and from there it is possible to reach, with practice, any shot. Take the shot, get back to the middle ready for the next one. If you get carried away and stay at the back, trying to manage all the shots from there, then you can back yourself into a corner. If you are at the front of the court it's impossible, without a lot of twisting and turning, to see what's coming at you from behind, and if it's a drop shot in the back corner you may not get there in time.

Your responsibility is to stay balanced, and the T spot is the place to be. I have found myself metaphorically running all over the court trying to help, trying to take responsibility for things that simply aren't my responsibility, and this is a key feature of the 6 Personal Year, and the 6 Life Path Number. The 6 wants to help, to serve, to be responsible. I have found myself stuck like glue to a situation that I don't actually want to be in, through leaving the middle of the court. The key to the number 6 energy is learning to balance giving with receiving, and finding where the point of personal harmony sits.

January in a 6 Personal Year puts you into a 7 month: a month to reflect, and I willingly step into a space I am familiar with. My tenants had mysteriously disappeared in the previous December, leaving me with a substantial deposit. They have, it would appear, returned to South Africa, leaving the flat and the garden in a mess, and I needed to get it back up to scratch ready for new tenants. I turn the radio on and start the process of cleaning, painting, and making good. There is a long to-do list. It is a strange and eerie feeling being back in my flat. The feeling of home has disappeared, and as I look around at what I had achieved during the renovation, I wonder whether running away from its loveliness in my 5 year was the right thing to do. I had created something very special without compromise, and was proud of my achievement. I remind myself that my decision felt right at the time, and in many ways it was. I was in receipt of additional money, as the flat I was renting was much cheaper, and this had giving me a lot more disposable income. I had enjoyed my time travelling and spreading my wings in my 5 year, and the extra money was of great benefit. But it is January, its freezing cold and I feel an unexpected sadness in my bones.

My vision of a beautiful home by the sea, where friends and family can come and be together seems like a distant dream. My new relationship has dragged me away to the idea of a different future, where we might be together despite our many differences. As I reflect on my previous relationships, I wonder why, in spite of all my efforts, I just can't seem to make things work. However, I am trying to play the part of myself within my new relationship, and I am learning more each day. But I sometimes find myself reading from an old script and stepping over old lines.

I had made a fundamental mistake in handing over a rather large file of paperwork to my partner. This was done towards the end of my 5 year, and at the time the sense of freedom was enormous. The papers were kept in a large box, and once they were out of sight, they became out of mind. I had accumulated the paperwork whilst at the flat, in the process of trying to unravel the mess that I had found myself in. There was a very short lease, something I had ignored due the fact that it was the perfect place to house my baby grand. My neighbour had persuaded me to support her in taking the chairman to court, in order to restore some harmony and order; but it felt like a constant battle that would never end. The associated paperwork had turned into a mountain. I had hoped that my partner would sort it out for me. However, the problem was thrown back when he became overwhelmed with it. My neighbours, who he had approached to try and resolve the situation, were true to form, rude, abusive, dismissive, and argumentative. The ball was clearly back where it should have stayed, in my court. My mess, my responsibility.

And so I step back up to the plate and relentlessly play the part of the peacemaker and diplomat. Surprisingly, to me, I do it rather well, and by the end of March the new lease is in the bag. It is a 9 Personal Month, a month indicating endings and the tying up of loose ends, and brings this particular piece of the jigsaw to a conclusion. This feels really good and like a huge achievement. It had taken months and months of stress and anxiety, and now finally it felt as if peace and harmony could be restored. The signing of the new lease also meant that my neighbour could move on, and her For Sale board is up in a flash.

After the concluding energy of March, April brings around a 1 month; a chance for new beginnings. Now that I had extended the lease it was my hope that I could sell the flat and buy a new home. With the piano gone I had more options. I also had a new tenant for a six-month period, and that reduced the stress of meeting the mortgage payment.

But there is a spanner in the works. At the suggestion that my new partner and I might consider living together sometime in the future, my youngest daughter announces that if that happened she wouldn't be living with me anymore. This expression of feeling was clearly distressing for her, and left me completely torn between my duty to her, and rightly or wrongly, my duty to myself. I had missed the companionship of a partner and was, in spite of its difficulties, glad to have another adult to talk to. However, the question of duty and family loomed large in the landscape of my 6 year. I resolved to try to be more receptive to what was being said, and use my energies to calm the waters. Things settle down but one set of duty and responsibility is replaced by another.

As I enter May, a 2 month, my diary shows a rebellion on the friend front. I have been absent due to my new relationship. It is easy to become totally immersed in a new relationship, to the exclusion of other things of importance, and clearly this had had an effect on my family and also my friends, and I am left feeling guilty. It's a bit of a wakeup call. I have a strong 1 vibration given my birthdate of 1st June, and once again I feel the dissonance of two numbers at odds with each other. The 2 energy requires us to put others first, to be receptive, the 1 insists on self. Once again I make adjustments and hope that the damage caused is not irreparable and that I have managed to re-balance and get back to the centre of my court.

Whenever I doubt my ability to be co-operative, diplomatic, and to act in the interests of partnership, I remind myself of my time spent building FASBAT. It was a most harmonious relationship giving us both the opportunity to play to each other's strengths. Astrologically speaking it was said to be the perfect mix of Gemini and Libra, two air signs flowing around in the atmosphere together. The energies seemed to be in sync. Whilst I flew around looking for a new discovery, my Libra partner searched for depth, and between us we managed to turn our business ideas into reality. We both developed creatively during this time, and after a couple of failed attempts, we had managed to cobble together enough people to run an adult class. The word had spread, and we finally increased our numbers enough put on a show. This took place in March, around about the same time that I had managed to increase the lease, and was called 'We Can Do It'. Once again the connection leaps out at me. It was a revue show and gave everyone the chance to show off their particular talent. They had arrived the previous September like rabbits in headlights, with stories of always wanting to sing, but being told they couldn't be in the choir, not getting into school plays, and generally feeling a lack of confidence in their ability to perform. But they did it, and they did it very well. They were no longer in the headlights, but in the spotlight, centre stage, strutting their stuff.

Later in the year the children's classes put on a performance of 'A Weekday Night at the Sunninghill Palladium'. I still have a broad smile on my face when I remember the phone call from my partner exclaiming 'I've got a great idea for the title of a show'. Given my memories of Sunday nights in Slough, I didn't stop grinning about the idea for days.

Obviously, the children were oblivious to the connection, but anyone of a certain age took a trip down memory lane, and we rejoiced in the ability of the 'Variety Show' genre to showcase individual talents.

FASBAT was family, and as our classes and reputation grew, we found ourselves firmly rooted to the community in which we were working. Our offering was extending to other schools in the form of after school classes, and pupils joined together in the special atmosphere of the theatre, where they bonded with each other and the magic of performance. Service was rewarded with happy faces and growing confidence, and this gave me a feeling of purpose, which far outweighed the monetary benefits. Our families often got involved serving behind the bar, putting out chairs, helping backstage and front of house. It was a wonderful feeling, and epitomised the energy of the 6, with the image of a mother nurturing her growing child. Family is everything to the 6 and I felt truly blessed on many occasions during the year as I worked to nurture my children, and also my business.

True to the synchronicity of the numbers, and its connection to love, marriage, and family, my son's engagement party takes place. My son and his intended have weathered the storm of meeting, just before his departure for Iraq in 2004, and they stand before us with their love secure, and ready to undertake the trials and tribulations of togetherness. The evening is fundamental to the idea of family. Our two families are very different, but there is an overwhelming feeling of love, as we mingle together to celebrate. I am faced with being in the midst of ex-husbands, and a new partner which is extremely testing, but the hope of new love gives an opportunity to put old feelings and hurt aside in the quest for peace and harmony. I am acutely aware that this is a difficult time for my youngest daughter, who is still struggling with the whole new partner situation, and the fracturing of our family unit. But the rest of the family close in, surrounding her with care, and I am overwhelmed with love for them all. They have weathered difficult situations like this before, and appear to have wisdom beyond their years. I feel my mistakes keenly during the evening, but I know that the only way forward is to carry on with the search to understand myself better, in the hope of eliminating mistakes based on lack of self-love and confidence in who I am.

The family is a social construct, and the saying that you 'choose your friends and not your family', is of course, a pointer towards familial duty and responsibility. There are families where all the energies supposedly flow together, in a never-ending stream of loveliness, and then there are families where the energies seem to collide into each other, causing distress, harm, and lasting damage. Physically giving birth to a child is a life-changing event for both mother and father. I remember as if it were yesterday, gazing down at my first born and being completely overwhelmed with a sense of responsibility and duty. It was a very daunting feeling, and I feel blessed that this sense has never left me, even though it acts as an irritant to my children when I overstep the line, and forget how independent they are. It is said of the number 6 that it should be like a well that people come to drink at, and not an empty pit where all the water had been emptied out leaving nothing to give. Beware of the line always. Give with all your heart, but learn to receive as well. When you go marching straight over the line you can become oblivious. Giving makes you feel good, so why not do more and more and more? If this rings a bell and you feel as if your well has run dry, take a moment to reflect. How can you receive if you are giving so much? Where is the balance? Without balance there is no harmony.

One of the most enlightening things I have ever read is by the Lebanese poet Khalil Gibran in *The Prophet*. It is a book of 26 prose poetry fables. It has been translated into 50 different languages and has never been out of print since its publication in 1923. When I first read it I was blown away by the profound quality of its writing, which presented me with new ideas about life, offering me a dogma-free universal spiritualism as opposed to orthodox religion.

In his writing 'On Children' he presents the following.

Your children are not your children.
They are the sons and daughters of life's longing for itself.
They come through you but not from you,
And though they are with you, yet they belong not to you.
You may give them your love but not your thoughts,
For they have their own thoughts.
You may house their bodies but not their souls,
For their souls dwell in the house of tomorrow, which you cannot
visit, not even in your dreams.
You may strive to be like them, but seek not to make them like you.
For life goes not backward nor tarries with yesterday.
You are the bows from which your children as living arrows are
sent forth.
The archer sees the mark upon the path of the infinite, and He
bends you with His might that His arrows may go swift and far.
Let your bending in the archer's hand be for gladness.
For even as He loves the arrow that flies, so He also loves the
bow that is stable.

Along with many others, his writing fed into my growing personal development during my 6 year, and also allowed me to take a fresh look at the idea of family. As parents we often try and impose our values and ideals onto our children, who act like sponges. We march straight in with balloons and trumpets and a very large megaphone. And we are so easily copied. The good, the bad, and the ugly. Many times during improvisation exercises at FASBAT we were treated to a performance of children acting out their parents, words and actions. In the immortal words of Stephen Sondheim 'careful the things you say, children will listen'. Of course if we view our children's behaviour as a reflection of ours, then it can be very distressing to see them disorganised if we are organised, non-communicative if we are communicators, and noisy if we are quiet. I now try to look at my children with different eyes, and see their amazing qualities in a whole new light. The 6 Personal Year is a great year to consider your responsibility to family relationships, and to balance it with your responsibility to self. It is the year to work towards balance and harmony for the good of all.

My children had only taken nine months to be created and come to fruition, and they all made a break for independence at roughly the same age. The elephant in my previous chapter, on the other hand, had taken many years to create, and had sat there determined not to leave the comfort of its home, hanging on like a parasite, refusing independence. I didn't realise it at the time, but the creation I had given birth to in Malta was to take a whole lot longer to come to fruition. It is only now as I am finishing writing this book some 17 years later, that I can see that some things take a very long time. A few seeds may germinate quickly, whilst others will take forever. If you plant a seed which grows annually it will germinate quickly. It will, with love, care, and fresh compost, continue to grow stronger every day, until it can be planted out to flower, and then fade within the period of a year. Each year within the numerology Epicycle can be seen as an opportunity to develop and grow, with each year bringing a different colour to life. The seed of knowledge from that year can then be harvested, and taken forward with you on your journey. If you plant an avocado seed, you will have to wait for months and months for it to germinate. The best way is to stick it in the soil forget about it. One day you will stumble across it, and be amazed by its fighting spirit and determination to be born, and they, like humans, can sometimes cover a lifespan of 100 years. If you have ditched a dream, it may still be there lurking around in the recess of your mind. If things are meant to be, then they will stick to you like an annoying piece of Sellotape which you can't seem to remove from your finger.

One of my favourite musical theatre shows is 'A Chorus Line'. It provides a glimpse into the personalities of the performers and the choreographer, as they describe the events that have shaped their lives and their decisions to become dancers. The theatre critic Michael Billington writes in *The Guardian Review* in 2013, of 'the permanent paradox of a Chorus Line: it hymns the individuals who are finally turned into glittering figures of anonymity'. As each performer steps into the spotlight they leave something with the audience, and in turn take something back; that is the way of the theatre, and also the way of life using numbers as a guide. We are able to step into the light of each new Personal Year using its energy to achieve wisdom. This can then be shared with everyone who steps onto our path. If the energy is used correctly in a 1 year it brings boldness, progress, and independence, it can have a positive effect as long as it hasn't tilted over to arrogance and rigidity on the one hand, or dependence insecurity and defeatism on the other hand. When you meet someone standing in the spotlight of the 4 energy, you may be met with reliability, organisation, and consistency, but when it steps out of the light it can become insensitive, slow, lazy, and unadaptable. The phrase 'happy in their own skin', is a phrase that can be applied to those beautifully balanced and enlightened individuals, who have reached a place of self-mastery, and this can be inspirational. But it is so easy to be upset and thrown by individuals, whether family, friends, or acquaintances who are rocking negative energies, and without balance we in turn, can have the same effect on them. When we take responsibility for the true expression of ourselves, without compromise, then we have the ability to harmonise and balance, bringing beauty and order into the world. It is a place where love grows in abundance. Our learning becomes like ripples on a pond, and is far reaching.

The 6 year vibration saw my interest in NLP and numerology developing. I felt pregnant with ideas; for me, a very satisfying part of the 6 energy. My baby was keen to be born, and I was excited to try out a numerology session, which would involve a group of friends getting together, so that I could give a talk on the subject, and then do some personal readings. A good friend obliged, and gathered together some interested individuals, who were keen to find out more about themselves. The gathering was peppered with some sceptical souls, who duly listened, and went away a little more knowledgeable about the subject. The evening and format were a success, and the more I ran these sessions and worked with a vast array of different people, the more I became amazed by the accuracy of this esoteric form of self-knowledge, and its ability to shine a light on our inner desires and talents, along with its power to help us develop independence, co-operation, creativity, etc.

Creative development continued to be a theme of my 6 Personal Year, and one of the most extraordinary experiences during this time sprang from a one day workshop I held, incorporating ideas for personal development, drawn from my own experience of the journey to date. This was held in a friend's studio in Wentworth, Surrey, and I spread the word by mouth, and also through posters in local shops. I received a phone call from a woman booking herself and her sister-in-law onto the course. I had asked everyone on the course to bring something to share for lunch, and they had duly turned up with their Tupperware boxes, and supermarket carrier bags full of goodies. The day before the course I had a call asking for directions. It was from a gentleman, and I was confused, as all the course members I had registered were female. When I queried this, he said he was calling on behalf of the Sultana. This threw me a little, and during a brief phone call to a knowledgeable friend, I was informed that we had members of a royal family living in our midst. We were greeted on the day with bodyguards, and an offer to provide lunch for all. This arrived in due course complete with china plates, silver service, and some of the most delicious vegetarian food I have ever tasted. The Sultana and her sister-in-law, fully engaged in every aspect of the course, revelling in the Blue Peter type exercise of cutting and pasting images from magazines onto a piece of card. These images act as a personal mood board for the things that are important to us. A very high-flying friend had passed this exercise onto me, saying that of all the many workshops he had been on, this was the exercise that had made the most difference. Good enough for me, and enjoyed by everyone I have ever presented with it.

Post course I was invited to lunch at what amounted to the palatial home from home, with a very close-knit group of personal advisors and gurus. This included a feisty and very beautiful Italian pilates instructor with a worldwide business. A serene and mysterious Scorpio yoga instructor. A Russian energy worker called Alla Svirinskaya whose book *Energy Secrets* I just couldn't put down, until I had consumed the whole of it' in one reading, and a very down to earth fitness instructor, who made me feel as if the dream I had wandered into was in fact real.

This all takes place in July, a 4 month in my 6 Personal Year. The 4 energy as always represents building, along with all its difficulties, and when placed alongside the creative development nature of the year, I felt certain that I was making good progress. The Russian, the Italian, and the Scorpio were an interesting mix of knowledge, wealth, and confidence, but for some reason my self-esteem took a huge knock and it felt, for a moment as if my newly built walls had been hit by a bulldozer, leaving the elephant smiling down at me eating a very tasty bun. They were all at the top of their game. We were all singing off the same sheet but placed next to them, I felt as if I just wasn't up to the mark, rather like a toddler who can almost walk, but can't quite do it with confidence. Their courses and businesses were all established, like graduating teenagers, but my baby was still in its infancy, and so I decided that the best thing I could do was just hang around in the wings and observe. Anthony Robbins speaks of modelling in his quest for self-mastery, and of accelerating the tempo of mastery by modelling. I felt blessed to be in the situation I had found myself, surrounded by some powerful role models, and as I quietly observed them, I could see that confidence was the common denominator. Their belief and passion about what they we doing matched mine, and I reminded myself that passion was included in my top five core values. I didn't have to be like them, anymore than I needed to be like my brothers, I just needed to be like me, and use my belief and passion to achieve success and confidence through what I was starting to do best.

I cried all the way home, but when the tears stopped, I was left with realisation that I had been there for a reason. I wasn't any less, or more than anyone else around the table. Our hostess clearly valued my input in the same way as everyone else. We all had different things to offer, and were all doing it in our own unique way. My fears were old fears – the ones I thought I had blown up and thrown into the gorge. Once I had got the wave back onto the shore, and it was gently flowing in and out, I realised that doing the workshop had given me valuable information on what worked, and what didn't, and further insight into the nature of fear. If I could remain confident then all would be well. I knew I had made a difference to the people attending the course, my number one core value, and that to me was the most important thing. I know that as long as I keep my core values at the centre of my existence, along with the information contained within my numerology, then my foundations will be/ should be indestructible.

In September, my 6th month in a 6 Personal Year, a month with double energy, I read an article about a soldier shot dead in Basra. It brings me to my knees. My detachment when my son was in Iraq had kept me sane. I had two choices, fall apart with worry, or try and hold myself together through detachment. I chose detachment and this had opened up a void. The duty, responsibility of care, and love that I felt for him had remained, and once again sweeps over me. I resolve to make an effort to communicate more. I want us all to spend more time together as a family, and when I hear that my Burleigh Wood House neighbours have sold, I make the decision to return home.

Before I moved out of Burleigh Wood and rented the flat above the Sun Cafe, I had become a regular, as it was in the village where my business was based. I had suggested a poetry wall so that customers could submit their words, and have them displayed for other people to read. This was taken on board and became a source of much talk in the village.

The following poem coincided with the Iraq war, and my 3 year of expression through writing. It seems curious that I had ended up living above the Sun Cafe for a period of time, as the feelings I couldn't express verbally to my son, I managed to express through writing, were there, placed on the wall as a testament to my love not only for my son, but for all mankind.

*The warm spring sun seeps through my skin and travels
to the centre of my body.*

A time for renewal… but that was yesterday.

*Today tears vacate my body, leaving an empty numbness,
as I awake to the sounds of war pervading
every wavelength.*

A war so far away, and yet so close to my heart

*A son, not yet called to fight, other sons
surrounded by the storm*

Mixed emotions tear at my consciousness, as my love

extends to all mothers who have given so much for so long.

Their decisions, our heartache…God be with them

May renewal come quickly allowing the sun back into the hearts of the nation.

My son had returned home safely, and it was now my turn.

I move back to Burleigh Wood House on 9th December, 2006 after a year of renewed family ties and growing creative development. I am immediately wrapped in its beauty and elegance, and in spite of the cold, pervading the impossible to heat Victorian splendour, I feel like a baby closeted in a warm embrace. The show title 'We Can Do It' from earlier in the year springs to mind, and I remind myself of my achievements throughout the year.

After a tricky start to the year, I had successfully renewed the lease, rescued some friendships, put my family at the centre, and grown my new baby… I did it! Dancing behind the sofa pretending to be a Tiller Girl once more becomes the exercise of choice for warming myself up, as I high kick my way towards a family Christmas, with everyone happily gathered back around the family table. I am surrounded by harmony (albeit it sometimes fractious and chaotic), but I am home again in the beautiful space which I had created with such love.

The information I had garnered during my studies around the Right Action had increased my awareness of what was possible during the year, and I felt as if I had managed to harness some of the energy to good effect. I leave the year feeling really quite pleased with myself!

YEAR 7:

THE ANALYST/SEEKER

Keywords: Reflection · Solitude · Scholarship

Underbalanced	**Right Action**	**Overbalanced**
dull		*distant*
vague		*detached*
uncertain	THINK	*stubborn*
ignorant	INTUIT	*impatient*
empty-headed	DIG DEEP	*reserved*
short-sighted	OBSERVE	*unresponsive*
	MEDITATE	
	INVESTIGATE	
	STUDY	

INTROSPECTION IS EVERYTHING

CHARACTER BRIEF
Seeker of wisdom, looking for the truth

Costume	Props
Sarong of Scholarship	Portable Cave
Philosophical Pyjamas	Wise Old Owl
Thinking Cap	Mirror of Mysticism

■ 7777777777777777777 ■

YEAR 7:

SOMEBODY FIND ME A CAVE

There is a sense of inner development, and a desire to specialise in one's line of work or talents. Introspection puts a small break between the activities. You may like to avoid crowds and socials this year and may concentrate, analyse, and meditate. This may lead to realisation and new lines of awareness. There is a waiting this year and a feeling of loneliness and detachment. Repression should be avoided.

Dr Ravindra Kumar
Secrets of Numerology

I am in a cave.
   The cave resembles a cathedral, but there are no stained glass windows, just an eerie light steaming in from the entrance. Under my feet I can feel the cold hard stone floor. I have hesitated at the door for several minutes, scared of what lies within, having arrived there after many years of avoidance. Now is not the time for turning back. It is time to go within and face the monsters. My feet have transported me to a long low ledge, and I obey the voice which fills the space urging me to sit down. The light creeps along the floor, swirls around my feet, then travels upwards and completely envelopes me. It is tinged with the colour of Lapiz, a deep blue; it gives me strength. As I sit there in the emptiness, I feel a strange sensation. My body feels light and there is a

tingling coming up from my toes. It travels towards my head, and when it has reached its destination, I become aware that my hair is starting to grow. The short hair which has adorned my head, trying to project an image of masculinity, since the distressing experience of being sat on the back kitchen table every couple of months, and having my locks cut off, is fighting back. But in this moment, I feel princess-like tresses flowing down to my shoulders. They don't stop there, they carry on down past my shoulder blades following the line of my spine, as they make their escape from the stunted confines of my messed up imagination. I feel my body expand. It's as if every organ in my body is singing. I am propelled upwards and immediately feel ten feet taller. As I regain my balance, I become aware of a pure white light coming in from the entrance. My flowing silver gown flaps behind me, dancing with my beautiful tresses, as I make my way back to the entrance of the cave. As I step into the daylight, a gentle breeze caresses my face, and I am met outside the door by two large snowy white wolves, who stay by my side as I journey back down the mountain. I am 54. It is 7th July: a 7 month in my 7th year of the Epicycle. It is a big moment.

Shamans come in all shapes and sizes. Mine came in the form of a bricklayer living in a tiny flat in Bagshot. As often happens, I had started chatting over a coffee with a complete stranger and found another soul in search of his truth. We talk above love, life, the spiritual journey, and above all, the desire to know ourselves better. He has just left a relationship, and is trying to find answers to all his niggling, unanswered questions. I relate. He has turned to astrology, crystals, Buddhism, and Shamanism. My knowledge of numerology has increased due to studying any book I can get my hands on, and I throw that into the mix; he listens transfixed as I describe his current Personal Year, mouth open. He tells me of his visit to a local Shaman, and his subsequent progress, despite having to go backwards to go forwards. He talks in terms of great strides and a sense of peace. I'm hooked. I return home and bury myself in books. I am alone for the weekend, and after two Sunday morning coffees, my head is buzzing with thoughts and imaginings. It is July, it is hot, and I spend a blissful afternoon in the shade surrounded by words, numbers, long cold drinks, and the sounds of birds chatting away in the oak tree.

You can imagine the number 7 with a rucksack on its back, laden with questions. The 7 seeks the truth, and will not rest until it has sought out the answers to life's greatest mysteries. We can of course collide with spiritual insight in any Personal Year, but the 7 is a very special number as far as spirituality is concerned, and this is why when you enter a 7 Personal Year, you are presented with such a wonderful opportunity to delve deeper into the mystery of yourself. According to Dr Shirley Lawrence in *The Secret Science of Numerology* 'The 7 turns its back on the upcoming numbers, and does not start the fervent work of the 8'. Pythagoras was known to have taken children with a 7 Destiny Number into his Mystery School, without first testing them, for the 7 meant they were born to pursue the course of spiritual enlightenment. I telephone the number on the crumpled serviette, make an appointment, and return to my imaginings, as I laze under the magical oak, which stands majestically waving its arms above me.

Thursday comes and I sit nervously outside the Shaman's flat, feeling a mixture of excitement and dread. He could be a mass murderer, he could be an escaped rapist, he could be a quack. But my Gemini twin kicks my misapprehension into touch, and assures me that the recommendation is sound. I gather my strength, walk up the path and knock at the door. As I sit in his dimly lit lounge, I look around at a collection of crystals, feathers and a large bookcase, groaning with spiritual literature. I relax as I start to feel at home. The question 'why are you here?' hits me square in the face. I tell him I have an interest in numerology. I blurt out that I am a number 7 and I am in a 7 year. I am not expecting him to know what I am talking about, but a broad smile creeps across his face, and I know instantly that we are on the same page. I am excited. We discuss my numbers in depth; I am stunned into silence and sit there with new ears. He tells me, that due to my preponderance of 5s I am likely to have many relationships. I feel vindicated, understood, and on the verge of something. I shuffle and wonder if he thinks he may be one of the many. But he is more concerned with the spiritual seeking of the 7, and expresses no surprise that I am here sitting in front of him, after a chance meeting, seeking his wisdom. I am led into a white uncluttered room with a single chair. As instructed, I sit down and close my eyes…

And so my journey into the cave began. I didn't know what I was looking for, or what would be coming towards me. I didn't know how I would feel afterwards. But clearly my subconscious did. I had never felt truly feminine, and had learnt to channel a tomboy persona. I am a very practical person and have no problem getting my hands dirty, and I love that about myself; but I am also deeply drawn to the word elegance which features on my list of core values, and this seemed to be in contradiction.

My hair, and my desire to be like my brothers, had always acted as a stumbling block in my mind. But it was clearly time for that to change. After my experience in the metaphorical cave of my mind, I felt altogether different. I suddenly felt connected to the whole; I no longer felt 'out of tune' with myself. I don't know why I was in the cafe at the time I was, meeting the person I met, being introduced to someone who could unlock my unconscious, but I do know that it was all connected. This happens all the time. Things connect up, we just don't notice until we start to pay attention. Would I have made that journey in a different Personal Year? Well yes probably, given that my Life Path is a 7 and unusual things seem to happen to anyone with that Life Path number, however, if you are not a 7 Life Path holder then you may find everything in your 7 Personal Year very strange. I have worked with many people who have thought they were 'losing the plot' in a 7 year.

Some of them party animals, who couldn't understand why all of a sudden they wanted to be on their own. Some of them quiet types, who felt they had fallen to the bottom of a large well, without the use of a ladder to help them back out. Whatever energy you are faced with on a daily, monthly, or yearly basis, the key is to relax into it. Giving yourself permission to retreat is needed in a 7 year, and communication of your desire to do this, is necessary to avoid dissonance. When the energy hits you respond in any way that you can. A half an hour sabbatical with the chance to contemplate your naval, is better than no sabbatical. It is easy just to try and push through these feelings, and not give in to them, feeling guilty or lazy, but if you can learn to do nothing 'with intent', you will find that it is a very satisfying experience.

Because of my now extensive reading around the whole idea of numerology, I had expected something significant to happen in my double 7 (Personal Year 7 and Life Path 7) and I wasn't disappointed. Finding a different perspective on the idea of 'feminine', has been a fundamental shift in my life, and has enabled me to look at the bigger idea.

Llewellyn Vaughan-Lee is a Sufi mystic and lineage successor in the Naqshbandiyya- Mujaddidiyya Sufi Order. He is an extensive lecturer and author of several books about Sufism, mysticism, dreamwork, and spirituality. He writes about the sacred feminine and explains it *as our sacred connection to life, that is present in every moment. It means to realise that life is one whole, and begin to recognise the interconnections that form the web of life. It means to realise that everything, every act, even every thought, affects the whole. And it also means to allow life to speak to us*.

It is not only books on numerology that I devour in my 7 year, but any book I can lay my hands on, which will help me connect more deeply to who I am. I just want to be holed up so that I can read and think and explore my heart and head. Stumbling across Deepak Chopra in my 7 year, and being introduced to the idea of 'pure potentiality further adds to the expansion of my idea of interconnectedness. He says, *'The source of all creation is pure consciousness ... pure potentiality seeking expression from the un-manifest to the manifest. And when we realise that our true Self is one of pure potentiality, we align with the power that manifests everything in nature...'*

He speaks of intention and attention. The phrase 'make your intention, and give it your attention', makes so much sense to me. Of course you need to know what is it you intend, but once you do, intention can be easily and specifically set within any Personal Year in the form of goals. These should be in line with the Right Action of the year. They can be simple goals, which tie in with the energy of each Personal Month, or a larger goal taking in the whole 12 months.

...*'Inherent in every intention and desire is the mechanics for its fulfilment ... intention and desire in the field of pure potentiality, have infinite organising power. And when we introduce an intention in the fertile ground of pure potentiality, we put this infinite organising power to work for us.'* We just need to hold the dream.

Of course sometimes it's hard to hold the dream, especially if there is resistance from those around you that you love. The 7 energy is strange and mystical, which can leave you floundering, and your nearest and dearest confused. After a 6 year when family, home, and friends are at the centre of your focus, a 7 year can leave you feeling lonely and disconnected, and on many occasions, I was to find myself feeling as if I was living on an entirely different planet from the rest of the world. Luckily, it was a feeling I am used to.

My 7 year had started with an all-girl skiing trip. It was a mixed bunch; mostly friends of friends, all of whom I had met at one time or another. I was making it my intention to develop my knowledge of numerology, by doing individual readings for anyone who was interested. Apart from one friend, who was very reluctant to accept my interest in anything esoteric, everyone was happy for me to spout my newfound knowledge; in fact, they seemed fascinated and encouraged by it. Talking about the subject in a group situation was compelling, throwing up all sorts of insights and revelations about individual hopes and desires. It was very satisfying to observe the connection between individuals, through numerology and astrology, and I am once again amazed by its apparent accuracy, especially regarding their individual Personal Years.

Generally people don't like change, they want you to stay just the way you are. This is what they are comfortable with. I could of course, have kept my newly found knowledge to myself, so as to not irritate the one friend, but I am a communicator, apparently with a tendency to 'preach', and I was feeling stoical. The word 'preach' had been hurled at me by the friend, and was bounced away by my sometimes arrogant nature, but after much thought I chose to take it as a compliment. The best dictionary fit of the word, and the one I would like to wear, is 'someone who earnestly advocates'. To me this indicates passion, and I am fine with that; although I know how irritating it can be when coming from the other direction. I take the point. But other people's reluctance to accept your change, is not a reason to avoid metamorphosis.

Whenever I hear the word preach, I am taken back to the Methodist Church I had attended every Sunday morning for many years. It was a big part of my younger life, and I found myself happy to disappear into the dark recesses of my mind during the long sermons, as words floated around the vaulted Methodist mansion, which I have come to think of as my very first cave. There were of course other people in my cave, which was filled from time to time with sometimes dissonant, but mostly harmonic sounds, as we sang hymns and gave thanks to an unknown and unseen being. There were long silences whilst people prayed, each disappearing into their own particular cave. It was mysterious, it was the day of rest – a meditation. Strangely it felt more like home, than home. They say that number 7s are spiritual vagabonds, and since my birth into Methodism I have dabbled with other religions, always seeking answers to my many questions. But I now find it difficult to sit through a service in a church, as any religious rhetoric, clashes with my expanded spirituality. But I remain grateful for the beauty found within the walls, and the silence I encounter when entering an empty building, as I do from time to time. The silence is different from any other silence, and it warms my soul. I remember as a 12-year-old being allowed into the pulpit, a place normally forbidden, to plead for funds for a Missionary project in South America. The congregation was very small, but the plight of the people in need of help spoke loudly to me, giving me the courage I needed to stand up and communicate, or indeed 'preach'. It was an early indication of my desire to have my voice heard, although at the time it was lost on me, due to the noise of my knees knocking together.

During my skiing trip I became very aware of the conflicting energies within myself. They have always been there; I just hadn't given them much thought. The desire to be in my own company, in silence, comes around very frequently, and is in stark contradiction to my need to communicate, causing upset and the impression of aloofness. I remember being in a ladies' toilet cubicle once, at around the age of 40, listening to a conversation two women were having about me. 'She keeps herself to herself, but when you actually talk to her she seems very nice, and really rather chatty.' This made me smile, and become aware that maybe I needed to be a) more approachable, and b) less talkative. There is always a balance to be found!

The first night of the trip finds me with a burning desire to be in a bedroom on my own. I was supposed to share, and I just couldn't. I took myself to the sofa, and was immediately at peace. Trying to explain your desire for retreat in a 7 year is sometimes difficult, and prone to misunderstanding, allowing self-doubt to take hold, due to the metaphorical shoulder monkey, questioning the validity of your innermost desires. You can feel selfish, out of order, and unkind communicating exactly what it is you need or desire; and of course this applies to many things. Despite my night-time retreats, which most people found strange and slightly amusing, I was immensely grateful to find myself in the company of open-minded individuals with whom I could converse. I am happiest and most alive analysing and discussing things in depth, and talking to people about their thoughts and ideas always brings me further clarity.

Another deeply inward journey I made in my 7 Personal Year, was through yoga and meditation. I had dabbled with it several times, but not really in any great depth. I had used it to stretch a few muscles rather than stretch my mind. I joined a local spa, mostly so I could sit in the steam room and hot tub, to warm myself up during the winter months, as my flat was freezing even with the heating on. There was a yoga class at a convenient time, and I decided to give it one more try. I found that I could disappear totally into myself, by closing my eyes and listening carefully to the instructions. I had previously kept my eyes open, and found myself easily distracted by everyone else in the class. But my new method seemed to work, and I found myself facing a far more fulfilling experience. Instead of my head becoming cluttered with thoughts about people who could bend further than me, had a nicer outfit, and had clearly been doing it for years, I managed to clear my mind, allowing the movement to become a source of meditation.

Spurred on by this small success, I decided I would dedicate some extra time to meditation. I was determined to make progress, and had a phrase, attributed to Pythagoras, ringing in my ears during the time. 'Decline from the public ways, walk in unfrequented paths.' I wasn't exactly sure what it meant, but I very much liked the idea of unfrequented paths, and I had a feeling I might find these through meditation. I had little desire to socialise during the first four months of the year, and I took to sitting in the middle of my large red chesterfield sofa facing the open fire. The fireplace was an original feature, which had survived the 1970s' re-development of Burleigh Wood House into flats, and provided a wonderful focus with its beautiful carving and red hot flames, dancing mesmerically in front of my eyes. I imagined that my thoughts would travel up the chimney and take me on a celestial journey. I saw myself cavorting around with the stars, dancing to the music of the spheres, whilst trying to solve the mysteries of the universe. Of course some days I had to give up. It was just too hard ... but on the days I did manage it – magic happened, as I disappeared into my breathing; just me and my connection to something vast and unending. The feelings of peace and wellbeing balanced my soul, and I returned to the world a better version than the one that had walked on the earth previously.

Wisdom doesn't always just rock up on your doorstep. I find you not only have to be open to it, you have to take action. The search for truth and wisdom is as old as man, and finding your very own inner wisdom or 'iWisdom' as I like to call it, can be helped along significantly, when you give yourself the space to incorporate silence into your world. A portable cave will come in handy in your 7 Personal Year, which may be in the guise of a bath, a quiet corner of a cafe, or the garden shed. The 7 needs time to rest, and I have found it is often under the influence of a 7 day or 7 month, that I become attuned to this need. When you feel the need to rest or reflect, do not ignore it. In all probability you might not be aware that you are having a 7 day, a 7 month, a 7 year, unless of course you are keeping a diary. You will just know. So follow your desire and inner knowledge. If you do not heed the warning the 7 energy has the ability to throw you on the floor: literally.

A very wise and intuitive friend I met recently, had not heeded the advice, and had carried on headlong into the left over creative development of her 6 year, trying to push forward with the completion of her educational programme. I had gone over her numerology with her at the end of the 6 year and flagged up the dangers of not listening to the Right Action principles of upcoming 7 year.

She knew intuitively that she needed to stop and take heed, to review her options, without any help from me, but she ignored her inner guidance, and the Right Action information, and ended up flat on her back with plenty of time to rest. She was irritated by the pushing aside of her collected knowledge, but was at the same time immensely grateful for the lesson, the sabbatical, and the time to reflect.

I had heeded the advice of Right Action during the year, and had made much progress spiritually. My fascination with numerology had grown exponentially, and I had deepened my knowledge about the subject through doing many readings, both individually and in groups.

However, it would seem that I had only been listening with one ear.

YEAR 8:

THE C.E.O.

Keywords: Achievement · Vision · Opportunity

Underbalanced	**Right Action**	**Overbalanced**
dishonest		*irresponsible*
weak		*unreliable*
lazy	EFFICIENCY	*unprincipled*
slovenly	PRACTICALITY	*rigid*
impractical	ENERGY	*selfish*
negligent	AMBITION	*possessive*
	SELF CONFIDENCE	
	SUSTAINED EFFORT	

APPROACH OPPORTUNITIES IN A BUSINESS-LIKE MANNER

CHARACTER BRIEF
Leader with ability to accumulate wealth

Costume	Props
Overalls of Organisation	Money Belt
Suit of Success	Abacus
Steel Toe Cap Boots	Cup of Capability

■ 8888888888888888888888 ■

YEAR 8:

MONEY MAKES

THE WORLD GO ROUND

After the introspection of last year, your Personal 8 Year feels more dynamic. If you have some large scale schemes, your 8 cycle can be a time to put them into practice. There is a danger that you could over-commit, so remember there are only 24 hours in a day. This is a year for hard work and considerable achievement, but if you overstretch yourself, you risk losing everything. Avoid getting into debt and relying on others. This is a good year to start a business either in partnership, or alone, and there is the potential to make a great deal of money if you remain sensible.

Teresa Moorey
The Numerology Bible

The 8 year is not a year to mess around. It means business, and I find myself with a lot on my plate. The number 8 is connected to the Capricorn energy, that wonderful no-nonsense, there's a job to be done and I'm going to do it energy. It is about achievement; financial and otherwise. I have Capricorn rising, and I love a bit of no-nonsense hard work; however, given that my Destiny number is a 7 – which is spiritual in nature, it causes a rub against the material nature of the 8.

Working out what your Right Livelihood is can take time. We are programmed to believe that hard work is all that is needed to make a living, and I know many people, who work their socks off to provide for themselves and their families. However, I also know many people who are wonderfully happy earning their livelihood, despite the fact that they spend as much time dedicated to work as everyone else, who have managed to make the work look more like joy than hard work. Of course for some it is the hard work which is joyful. Buddhism defines the term Right Livelihood with regard to ethical employment; work that doesn't harm the planet or the people inhabiting the planet, and this is a sound idea. However for the purposes of this chapter, I am using this very useful term, to explore a much more personal look at livelihood, and what is right for the individual as defined by numerology. Having the courage to follow this knowledge can be troublesome, especially where fear and social pressure steps in, and sometimes circumstances take you away from what you know is right.

My 8 year starts and ends with a list: it is to be the year of lists!

In a year where the essence is achievement, a list is a very good thing. It always feels satisfying when you cross something off a list, even a small achievement. However it didn't look as if I was going to be crossing things off very quickly, as they each looked like mammoth tasks.

· Finish Trelawney House
· Finish Studio – rent out
· Finish Burleigh Wood House
· March – Talent show
· Develop Programme and Personal Philosophy Workshops
· Seaside Special/Rosie's Bar/Quiz?

Some people seem to know from the word go what is right for them. They appear to just get on the path and stay on it, floating through life in a state of happiness, leaving their time on earth content with their achievements, empire, family dynasty, contribution to society, or whatever it is that floats their boat. However, many of the people I have had the pleasure to work with, have made the comment 'when I was younger I always wanted to...'. Many years later they are left searching for answers to assuage their dissatisfaction and ameliorate their health issues. Our bodies are amazing barometers for disease, or as I have seen it described dis-ease. If we are not listening to our higher selves, our inner intuition, or gut feelings, or whatever you want to call that 'thing' which we so often dismiss, then we can end up in a bit of a pickle. If this is where you are – in a bit of a pickle, then you have excellent leverage for change.

The path is always there; it may be covered in debris and hardly discernible, but it is always there, and so are the side roads, and that's ok. Getting on the path is one thing, staying on it takes a whole different set of skills, including courage and trust. But the more you learn to trust yourself, your inner reference, instead of outer reference, i.e. advice from friends, family, the media, the internet, etc. the more you will tune into your inner wisdom. Things take time, and there is always a reason for the diversions, a lesson for you to learn along the way, or maybe something for you to pass on to someone else.

My previous year had taken me to some weird places; places I was actually very comfortable in. But standing in my 8 year they felt like a dream. Mystical meanderings turned into material must-dos.

Matthew Goodwin writing in the *Complete Guide to Numerology Volume 1*, states '*For a number 7* (which of course you know by now I am), *desire for material accumulation will probably lead the individual off track*'.

Hindsight. What a wonderful thing.

I felt there was a ticking clock behind me all through my 8 year. Post-divorce, I had an agreement to receive financial support, for the duration of my youngest daughter's journey to 18, a number which would curiously coincide with the end of this particular epicycle. This was fast approaching, and although I craved my independence I knew that the business I was involved in, would not allow me to fulfil my dreams, let alone keep a roof over my head, well my rather grand Ascot head anyway. My Total Expression Number (a number derived from all the letters in your name) is a 22 – Master Builder and I like to think big. But it's a tricky number. I had visions of FASBAT Franchises all over the country. The business provided me with an income, and I had been pushing to expand the offering to increase this, but my business partner and I were not quite on the same page. She very sensibly wanted to grow the business organically, and at a slower pace, but our financial situations were very different, and therefore I was coming from a different angle. Our passion for the business was equal, and I was aware of the theory that you shouldn't go after skyrocketing expansion if you want to survive long-term. But I am an ideas person, and was always trying to come up with new ideas to make money; to expand and build. We had already increased our presence in local schools, and were now delivering four shows a year, but for me it wasn't enough, and I was keen to continue developing my idea for an extended Personal Philosophy Programme, to run alongside the Musical Theatre Business. This desire was coming from my heart, and not the daily glances at my bank balance, and it felt right. However, there was the recurring question of the roof over my head and my dreams. I absolutely loved my flat, it was full of me-ness. I was surrounded by decisions I had made without reference to anyone else, and with sufficient money to accomplish the desired look. It represented my independence, despite the fact that I was not yet fully standing on my own two feet. The budget had run out and I was now in the position of maintenance of life on a daily basis.

I had grown ever fonder of the creaky old place during my 7 year, and my children loved coming over for lunch, and sitting on the large bench in the garden sharing family time. My daily walk around the garden, a place that I had put my heart and soul into, filled me with joy and anchored me to the space. My new neighbours had made all the difference to my experience of being there, and I loved them like family. We were fighting the difficulties together, and this was a source of comfort; I no longer felt out on a limb. I had taken the lead, given my knowledge of the complicated situation, and this felt much better than the feeling of abdicating my responsibility, or letting my previous neighbour make all the running. However, I oscillated between wanting to stay, and wanting to sell the place to ease my financial situation. Having increased the terms of the lease in my 6 Personal Year, I had tried to sell it in my 7 year, but there were no takers, and so I was back wanting to make the most of it and stay.

I am good at restoration, and the combination of my love of the practical, my eye for design, and my builder tendencies had been noted by my business partner. She was aware of her need to grow the business slowly, and also my need to make more money post-divorce. I thought that property developing would be a good way to increase the coffers, and could easily run alongside my other business, and she agreed to support this. I decide to go ahead and seek the advice of a Financial Advisor. Before the purchase he did a very good job in pointing out that it might be a risky thing to do, as he sensed a certain uneasiness in the market, but I felt confident in my abilities to pull off a good refurbishment and make a profit.

I had no problem whatsoever increasing the mortgage by a significant amount, due to the capital in the building, and everything seemed new and exciting. When I take myself back to the moment when I signed on the dotted line (and it is a moment I can thankfully get to very effectively), I know that there was something inside me saying NO, this is not the Right Action. But I didn't listen to my inner wisdom, that was telling me to concentrate on developing my Personal Philosophy Programme, and to educate myself further in the art of numerology. My financial situation was at the forefront of my mind, and I knew I had to take some sort of action if I wanted to continuing living at my flat, and work towards my dream of my other house by the sea. I had a lot of equity in the flat and I borrowed enough money, not only to buy a second house, but also enough to build a studio at the bottom of the garden, leaving me with a very large mortgage and an enormous amount to do.

By March, the studio was completed, and due to an increasing concern about money I rent it out to a friend. It had been extremely stressful trying to get it finished, but my son, a builder had stepped in to save the day, despite his very heavy workload. I had dreamt up the idea of a studio in my 7 year, and had wanted it to be a place of retreat amongst the trees. A place to do yoga, a place to just be, but now there wasn't any time for that. The number 8 means business, and daydreaming had to take a back seat.

By May, and to my great relief, the second house was completed, once again with the help of my son. It looked amazing, and after a week on the market I had received five offers. The offer I accepted would have given me a very healthy profit, which I had intended to plough back into another property, with the idea of using further profits to reduce my mortgage debt, enabling me to stay at Burleigh Wood House; but it was the year of the banking collapse and Lehman Brothers went bankrupt.

Merrill Lynch, AIG, Freddie Mac, Fannie Mae, HBOS, Royal Bank of Scotland, Bradford & Bingley, Fortis, Hypo, and Alliance & Leicester all came within a whisker of doing the same, and had to be rescued. Writing in *The Guardian*, Nick Mathieson recalls *'that 2008 started in a mood of eerie calm, but then exploded into global financial earthquake'*. The building societies and banks battened down the hatches against the oncoming cloud of doom. Everyone was struggling to obtain a mortgage, and the offers on the house disappeared. I made the decision to rent in the meantime to cover the mortgage, in the hope that the market would recover. I spend another two exhausting weeks furnishing the house, to get it ready for a rental market with a preference for fully furnished. Luckily, my daughter is very good with a flat pack and a screwdriver, and in spite of her reluctance, we managed to get it all done very quickly. This proved to be fruitful and I manage to secure a year's contract.

Despite the difficulty and rub of my 8 Personal Year, there were moments of utter joy. One being in the midst of what I now think of as the 'eerie calm' before the storm. The refurbished property was in Langley, on the outskirts of Slough, my hometown. The geography is such that in order to get from Ascot to Langley, you need to go through the Queen's back garden, Windsor Great Park. In the cold January mornings when I couldn't sleep, and was getting up at 5.30, to do some work on the house, before rushing back to take my daughter to school, I was often greeted by the painfully beautiful sight of the great oaks trees, which line the route across this most wonderful landscape visited by sparkling white frost. They sat in a low lying mist, like spectres shining in the darkness, and reduced me to tears on more than one occasion. Despite my feelings of exhaustion, the sight of the trees seemed to ground me, making it feel good to be alive. They just stood there being the best trees they could be, individually and together, feet planted firmly on the soil, revelling in their 'treeness'. I reminded myself that I was blessed. My life was full. I was getting to spend more time with my son due to his involvement in the building work, I had a plan, and I appeared, at the time, to be making financial progress. But the hard physical work did not bring me much joy, just aching joints and fitful sleep. Despite this I felt satisfaction every time a job was ticked off my large to do list, and I could see that the end result would be a beautiful transformation. I was using many of my talents, and in a way what I was doing was making a difference, as someone would end up with a lovely home. I thought all was well.

Little did I know what was to follow.

I had been aware of the significance of the number 8 energy, and its connection to all things material, but I had not studied it in enough depth. There was a number 8 in the year (2008), and I had named the new company set up to do the development 'No 8 Properties', and I would be finishing the project and hopefully raking in the profit in my 8 Personal Year. The 8s had it. I knew a lot of people who rocked the number 8, either as a Destiny Number or a Birth Day Number, and for the most part they were extremely successful and very good at business. I was convinced that I could do the same in my 8 Personal Year, what I hadn't quite grasped, was the dissonance and chaos that my opposing numbers would wreak. I know now, and I am grateful for the lesson. It was probably one of the biggest and most powerful examples of leverage in my life to date. The 7 Life Path is about the accumulation of wisdom and understanding, not money, and curiously enough in the end, the loss of the money didn't actually phase me. My diary entry of the 14th May, 2008 shows me feeling philosophical. 'It has clarified one thing for me, I need to use my analytical brain more and desire for knowledge and not my body. I must take care of my body and not abuse it.' The profit it would appear for me was in the lesson.

I had been in the throes of the menopause since the middle of my 7 year, and the physical exertion needed to finish the studio, complete the refurbishment, undertake my share of the work at FASBAT, engage in the difficulties at Burleigh Wood House, which still hadn't gone away, had all taken their toll; but I had decided that it was all just physical and survivable, and so I just ploughed on, conveniently forgetting the feelings of pain and exhaustion. It was a little like giving birth. Once the baby is there, despite the labour involved, you just have to carry on.

However, there was another force at work when it comes to the physical use of my body. I have since realised, because I still do it now on occasions, that I use my physical body to avoid using my brain. I have always had a very annoying habit of moving my furniture around, especially when there is something I need to focus on, quite often damaging my back or causing some other part of me to become disabled. This had been a recurring theme. Part of it is fear of failure, part of it is scattered energy, part of it the urge to create a little more order in my world. We all have our ways of avoiding things, and normally for me they only have a slight impact, but this time I had thrown my body at something physical instead of mental, and lost a significant amount of money to boot.

However, doing the house felt much easier than addressing the work required to build a Personal Philosophy Programme, which was work of an entirely different kind. My repeated avoidance technique was very tiresome, as I know when I do make myself sit down, and focus on using my brain instead of my body, things just unfold, ideas come to me, and I get lost in the flow. Hard work which turns into a much deeper sense of achievement. I may not have been phased by the loss of the money, but I felt extremely distressed by the idea of the waste, and I was angry with myself for going against my instinct, and not drawing on what I had learnt about myself to date; but some lessons take longer. And one thing is for sure, they will keep turning up on your doorstep until you have learnt the lesson.

Money is a tricky thing, and the number 8 and its energy, is the number that I have had the most difficulty understanding, as it feels a little alien to me. Even when I've been broke, I've had enough. Money always seems to turn up, sometimes just in the nick of time. When I've had more money than I need, I find that in some ways it saps my creativity, and I find myself buying things just for the sake of it. I seem to prefer the challenge of make do and mend. Don't get me wrong; I like to buy lovely things for my home and family, and I like to travel given any opportunity. I love the theatre and entertaining, and I like a healthy bank balance. I have always made a living, but I have never had an overwhelming desire to accumulate wealth. But some people do, and they are extremely good at making money; and that's ok, but that was not my path. As with all things there is always an upside and a downside. Money can be squandered or used for good purpose. But it is a fact of life and our connection to it, and the way we earn it is crucial to who we are. I believe there is a natural flow when you are engaging in 'Right Livelihood'; the right way to make money, by using your talents and abilities with love and passion.

I did some numerology with a very talented doctor I met whilst at a spiritual retreat in Wales. She had a number 8 Destiny Number, but she was struggling with the whole idea of money. She was adamant and uncomfortable about having more money than she needed saying, 'that's not what makes me tick'. But she talked about building a Healing Centre for people down on their luck, so that they could be ministered to, in a compassionate and caring way, even if they did not have money. She seemed offended to hear that her Destiny Number was an 8 – rather like my business partner, also an 8, who would have felt more comfortable paying people to come to our classes, rather than the other way around.

I suggested that she may need to balance her ideas around money. She was bright, intelligent, and passionate, and clearly had everything needed to succeed, but her limiting ideas of how money works was standing in her way. She was taking it personally, and it was interfering with her desire to do good, which for her far outweighed any monetary gain. In order to achieve her dream, she needed to be at peace with the power that the material can have when used for good. After many hours talking around the subject with myself and others at the retreat, she started to see her Destiny Number 8 as a blessing and a gift that she had been given, instead of a curse. She realised that she needed to combine all of her talents to achieve her dream, including her ability to make a significant amount of money. Her Motivation Number was a 9 – the number of compassion and humanitarian pursuit, and this caused a dissonance when placed against her ideas around material gain.

Joanne Walmsley of Sacred Scribes describes the number 8 as the 'Power Number' which needs always to be used for the good of mankind. The task of the 8 is great – and when awakened and developed, is the 'Master Energy' working for humanity.

Edna Adan Ismail who was born on 8th September, 1937 in Somalia, has been hailed as the 'Muslim Mother Theresa'.

Edna saw first-hand how poor healthcare, lack of education, and ancient superstitions had devastating effects on Somaliland's people, especially its women. When she suffered the trauma of FGM (female genital mutilation) herself as a young girl at the bidding of her mother, Edna's determination was set. The first midwife to practise in Somaliland, Edna became a formidable teacher and campaigner for women's health. As her country was swept up in its bloody fight for independence, Edna rose to become its First Lady and first female Cabinet Minister.

Edna sold everything she had, and built her own hospital brick by brick, training future generations in what has been hailed as one of the Horn of Africa's finest university hospitals. Edna's birth day is an 8, her month of birth September, the 9th month – I always refer to the 9 as the Mother Theresa number, as it is the number of the humanitarian. It also resonates with the astrological sign of Virgo – a sign associated with healing, service, and communication. Her Life Path Number is a 1, the number of the Pioneer, Strong Leader, and Independent Thinker. To me she stands as a fascinating example of the insights to be gained through numerology, in relation to how we command 'Right Livelihood'. The combination of her numerology and astrology, has clearly been put to good use to help the plight of humanity.

Of course we can't all make such a difference on a world stage, but we can in our everyday lives, by being true to our inner calling. If you have become deaf to that calling, then analysing your numerology will help you find a way to listen differently.

My understanding, after losing a large amount of money in my 8 year, was enlightening, and significant in my forward movement. I was starting to understand, that however scary it was, I needed to follow my heart and to receive compensation from the right source. As Kahlil Gilbran so eloquently writes *'to love life through work is to be intimate with life's innermost secret'.*

I feel my power and authority most, when I am engaging in activity which vibrates with my Core numbers; and this brings me peace.

Life Path Number	7	Analysis
Soul Urge /Motivation	6	Service, Balance, Harmony
Expression	22	Master Builder
Birthday	1	Independence, Innovation, Leadership

When you are in the flow you seem to lose all sense of being in the world, and to me that feeling is very spiritual in nature. It feels as if time passes you by, or stands still. I can lose myself for hours, in something requiring in-depth analysis and understanding, which then feeds into my creativity, which gives me the ability to build. I love to do this independently and quietly. When this happens I feel completely at one with the Universe, and it is only when I come back into a different state, let's call it a worldly state, that fear kicks in, and I start to doubt myself, and my ability to achieve something which will make a difference to people's lives. And that's when I go off at a tangent and start developing houses instead of developing programmes.

Several times I have been into a cafe, and been served by someone who clearly is not happy doing their job. There is no eye contact, no connection, and no passion. I have also been attended to by someone who loves to serve; it just flows out of them. I was knocked out whilst on holiday, in a tiny cafe in the middle of Lanzarote by someone clearly manifesting 'Right Livelihood'. Her Destiny Number was 6. I was so taken by her enthusiasm and apparent love of what she was engaged in, I had to ask her date of birth, and, as predicted, her attitude matched the energy of her numerology. I didn't think to ask the former, but I don't have to tell you that the coffee didn't taste as wonderful as the coffee served with love, enthusiasm, and purpose. It was an enlightening moment, and I seem to have been asking people what their date of birth is ever since!

I return again to the poetry of Kahlil Gilbran when he writes:

Work is love made visible
And if you cannot work with love but only with distaste,
it is better that you should leave your work and sit at the gate of
the temple and take arms of those who work with joy.
For if you bake bread with indifference, you bake a bitter bread
that feeds half man's hunger.
And if you grudge the crushing of the grapes, your grudge distils
a poison in the wine.
And if you sing as angels, and love not the singing, you muffle
man's ears to the voices of the day and the voices of the night.

It was such a joy to receive service from someone who rejoiced in her daily work with such love.

Post financial hiccup my year moves on at a pace. The Crown Estate held the head lease for Burleigh Wood House, which used to be on Henry VIII's hunting route, and although they had passed the day to day running of the house to the Burleigh Wood House Management Company, they were aware of the problems. I had been to the Crown Estate offices many times to try and engage their help, which they were unable to give (although the tea and biscuits were first class), and had sat there in tears trying to find a solution. A charming surveyor had eventually taken to my plight, and that of my neighbour, who had accompanied me to our final meeting, and informed us of new legislation designed to protect the rights of tenants. As long as at least 50 per cent of the tenants were willing, a Right to Manage Company could be set up to take over the running of the Management Company. The maths worked; there were four flats, and myself and my new neighbours were beyond willing. The chairman of the Management Company had control of three votes. His own, flat number (2) the proxy vote he held for the missing person in flat number (4), and his casting vote as chairman. We stood no chance of resolution with this 3/2 vote combination, and so at the end of May 2008 we started the process of setting up a Right To Manage company, which would allow myself and my neighbour the opportunity to take the power back. Power and authority are two of the words associated with the number 8 which I hadn't really connected to, as power isn't usually a word which I take much notice of. But as always, the intervention seems to come at just the right moment.

DIARY ENTRY
27th MAY, 2008 – ASCOT

I can't go on like this but I just have to keep on going in an effort to clear all this rubbish out of my life. Burleigh Wood is bringing me to my knees. I just want to go to sleep and wake up to find something different, something worthwhile. Something I can love that loves me back. I can feel it in my bones that I am heading towards a major change. I reflect on the last eight years of my life which have been filled with so many emotions; joy, sadness, stress, excitement, development, uncertainty, friendship, but most of all growth. I have steadily grown towards independence. I anticipate a few more hurdles, but I am hoping that I can face them in the flow.

My diary of 2nd June sees another list clarifying my desires, and questioning what I did want and what I didn't want going forward. I was aware that I was coming towards the end of a nine-year cycle, and I was starting to look forward to the possibilities of the next one.

WHAT I DON'T WANT DURING THE NEXT NINE-YEAR CYCLE

Burleigh Wood House
Scattered energy
No energy
Chaos

WHAT I DO WANT

Focus/direction/Right Livelihood
Passion
Recognition
Health/energy/vitality
Peace

My feelings of self-empowerment were growing, and I could at last see a light at the end of the tunnel. I started to think about the words 'power' and 'authority' differently, and started to see the 8 year as an opportunity to stand in my own personal power and authority. I needed to stand strongly rooted in my true self, just like the trees in the Great Park. I hoped that the mist would clear, and the way would become apparent. I felt a little alone in the mist, but knew that somewhere behind the clouds the sun was still shining.

I decide on a course of action in the wake of my refurbishment fiasco enlightenment, and decide to take a risk, this time one that seemed to hold so much more fear than refurbishing a house and losing money. I approach the Headteacher of my daughters school, to see if she would consider me running a trial Personal

Philosophy Workshop just before the end of term. She agrees, and I spent several happy and fulfilling days, pulling my ideas together and putting them into a suitable format. It wasn't perfect by any means, but it was progress. The successful completion and very complimentary feedback takes me forward into more creative development work in July, a 6 personal month in my 8 year. I feel like a pregnant woman, and my ideas are growing thick and fast. I have no desire to move anything, physically build anything, or hoover which is a blessed relief, and I make significant progress.

I plan another workshop session with an older group during the summer holidays. Above all I wanted to include numerology and astrology in the workshop, alongside the mainstream personal development exercises. I was aware of the controversial nature of this, but having cleared it with the parents, I find the girls fascinated by the information. Some of them chose to use it when considering their core values, the things that really matter to them, and this was followed by a hearty discussion regarding their upcoming A levels choices. This felt like something really worthwhile, and I loved every minute of the workshop. We build a large circle on the floor, dividing it into sections with masking tape, and examine the different areas that make up life. They reflect on where they are, and where they want to get to, grapple with their core values and devour every scrap of information. They welcome the opportunity to discuss these things in a group setting and help each other with their outcomes. As they stand in line to present their personal findings, stepping forward one by one into the spotlight, I feel a sense of wellbeing which I only really get when helping people to analyse, discuss, and discover.

August is spent happily getting the flat and garden up to scratch, having neglected it in the early part of the year. FASBAT is finished until September and the break is welcomed with open arms. We had completed three shows during the year with one left to do in the December. Our new venture earlier in the year was our first production of FASBAT Has Talent. It was a huge success, with all the pupils able to perform whatever they felt showed off their best talent. Risks were taken. We had dancing, poetry, comedy, singing, and drama. Some pupils had directed pieces, and some had written and performed their own work. Seeing an audience leave a performance with beaming smiles does it for me every time. Every child was supportive of each other and the confidence they had gained in their weekly classes shone through. Some pupils, decided they hadn't chosen their best talent, and tried something different the year after. They all drew inspiration from each other, and went on to develop and build from their own inner desires, to perform to their highest abilities. When I look back and reflect on the best use of my talents during my 8 year, I can see that although we are all capable of many things, identifying the talent which makes your heart sing the loudest, and that most closely matches your core values and heart's desire, is worth the disappointments and delays on the road to personal development and self-mastery. I had spread myself far too thinly, and in the wrong direction, and during this time a phrase kept popping into my head, which I had heard from the lips of a very successful and dynamic Vice President I had worked for before moving to Ascot. The phrase 'do less better' was conjoining with my desire to concentrate on my numerology studies and programme development. But the financial pressure remained, and I was determined to change the situation I had manoeuvred myself into so that I could make this happen.

DIARY ENTRY
8th AUGUST, 2008 – (888) – ASCOT

Maybe today I should finalise the plan in my head for financial security – maybe I should just trust that it will be OK. I guess

I just need to do what I do best, and continue in the direction of my dreams.

It is the anniversary of my father's birthday, and I sit, cappuccino in hand, reflecting on his life. Harold Flynn was born on the 8th August 1908, (888), and it was not until very recently that I realised his Life Path Number was the same as mine, a 7; 8.8.1908 = 34/7. It was there all the time, I just hadn't done the math, or indeed noticed that there was a wise old owl sitting right in the corner of the lounge, right in front of my eyes. Many things weren't talked about during my childhood. I was a child who listened behind doors, needing to assuage my need for information, however the subject of money seemed to be talked about freely and constantly and within my earshot.

My father and mother had left Hartlepool due to lack of work. I remember stories of my father collecting coal on the beach, riding 20 miles a day on his bike in the hope of work, and of struggling to keep a roof over their heads by any means possible. Times were indeed hard. His passion however, in these dark times, was horse racing. My much older brother, who was party to so much more of my parents' earlier life, tells the story of my father running a gambling business after their move to the south. It was illegal at the time, but he was apparently very good at it, employing several bookies' runners to cover the fast growing Slough estates, taking bets and organising the business. It was a precarious occupation and my brother recalls never knowing whether it would be a good Christmas or a bad one. But my father had managed a) to avoid jail, and b) to amass a stake large enough to join with two other gentlemen, who were to form one of the first legal betting shops. Betting shops became legal in 1961, with 10,000 opening up around the country within the first six months. But he lost the whole of his stake when an outsider called Psidium romped in at 66/1, leaving him unable to take part in the venture. Illegal bookmakers were common before betting became legal, and Stan Hey tells of a similar story writing in *The Independent* in 2008.

'My father worked for English Electric in Liverpool, a vast factory on the East Lancashire Road that in the late Fifties/ early Sixties employed around 15,000 workers. One summer night, when I was about eight, he took me for a ride in his Ford Popular from our house in Dovecot to an art-deco pub called The Bow & Arrow in the sedate suburb of West Derby. He left me in the car for a moment as he went inside, carrying a small bag. I saw more cars pull up and more men go inside. Moments later, a scene reminiscent of the Keystone Cops ensued, as men fled from the pub, with many of them jumping out of windows.

I never did find out exactly what had happened that night, but my best guess is that a delivery of punters' money was taking place to a bookmaker when tax officials decided to make a raid. I had clearly been used as a decoy, as no one would suspect a man with a small child in tow of such skulduggery.

The fact that one of dad's best friends at the factory left to set up two betting shops, and for whom he went to work as a settler (the person who works out the winnings of a bet) on Saturdays, convinced me that they had been in cahoots as runners inside English Electric. (I should also add that there wasn't a family holiday that didn't take in a trip to a racecourse en route.)'

As far as I know I was never used as a decoy, but I certainly remember spending many happy hours at racecourses as a child, especially Ascot, collecting the colourful betting tickets with my cousin Sally, and playing racecourse snap. My brother speaks of our father's quick mind and amazing mathematical and analytical ability. He loved to analyse the odds and knew every horse in every race, along with their form.

My mother had come from a middle class family, and had fallen in love with my father who was firmly working class. He voted labour, she voted conservative. There were difficulties. But he was a very dashing Leo with a lust for life and financial gain, and in spite of her recalling the passing over of another certain gentleman of the same class as her, she clearly adored him. They met on bonfire night, very apt for a pair of fiery Leos, and had stuck by each other for more than 60 years, through all the hardships that they suffered; and there were many. My father, in spite of his 888 vibration never made his fortune, but always provided for our family. I don't really know, but I can only imagine that his 7 Life Path Number rubbed against his number 8 Birthday Number, making for a constant struggle. He clearly wasn't meant to make a million. I remember finding him sitting in the lounge one day just before he died, with his building society book in his hand. He commented to me that all was in order, and that he could now die knowing that he could pay for his funeral, and there would be money there for my mother to carry on without him. He died shortly after leaving a huge hole in my life. I would love to sit in that lounge now with him and talk about his life and struggles. If only I knew then what I know now, I would have cherished him more, stayed longer, and listened to the wisdom he has garnered through life vicissitudes. I still imagine him riding his bike up to the betting shop, or sitting in his favourite armchair pondering life, rather as I do when I am lying in the bath or walking along a cliff path.

But you don't seem to know these things when you are young. I couldn't wait to leave the family home when I was 17, curiously a number 8 house. I escaped to London, taking up a position at the Methodist Missionary Society. I'd had the immense pleasure of knowing an Industrial Chaplain during my time at Coopers

Mechanical Joints, the place I went to straight from school at the age of 15, and where my father worked in the Despatch Department. I worked as a junior in the Accounts Department, until sexually harassed by a rather large, balding, and bombastic accountant. I had yet to stand in my power and authority. I complained to the Personnel Department and was swiftly moved to Stock Control, where I was looked after by a comforting group of mother hens. It was a rather wonderful old-style Engineering Company, and juniors were moved around from department to department, to gain experience of the whole business. Ironically, I ended up in the Personnel Department, where I would regularly put calls out over the tannoy requesting that Father (Alan) Christmas, report to the Personnel Department. I did of course always leave out his Christian name. Oh the joy of that tannoy and the feeling that it gave me.

However, I was still living at home, and I needed an adventure. My heart was telling me that there was more for me out in the big wide world. My father had put aside his dreams, and had steadfastly worked to support his family, remaining in the company for 20 years, thereby receiving a much treasured gold watch. I loved my father dearly, and liked to visit him at lunchtime, but we were not allowed to eat in the same canteen, and so we ate our jam sandwiches, a firm lunchtime favourite, in his office at the back of the factory. I can still smell the musty aroma of the office to this day; it was our little cave. I knew nothing of numerology then and had no idea that his Life Path Number was the same as mine. I just knew that we were happy tucked away in our little corner of the world, silently eating our jam sandwiches. He was only allowed into the 'works' canteen, and I was only allowed into the 'staff' canteen. The segregation continued with the Managers Canteen, and the Directors Dining Room. How things have changed. I clearly remember my incredulity at the rules and regulations, including the fact that females were not allowed to wear trousers to work. I think my fighting spirit and ideas about justice must have taken seed there. I deplore injustice, but felt completely powerless to change anything. However, I am now happy to stick my head above the parapet given an unjust situation, and I am thankful for my time in the midst of such ridiculous inequality. I was proud of my father's achievement, but the thought of doing anything consistently for 20 years filled me with horror. Father Christmas understood my predicament, and suggested the he used one of his contacts to enable me to apply for a position in the wider world. I had an association with the Methodist Church, having attended since the age of 5 – going to Sunday School and eventually teaching the younger children. Although the position was in London, the fact that it was the Methodist Missionary Society seemed to provide a sense of safety and family. I took up my position as an Audio Typist/Secretary in September 1971 – a 7 month in a 7 year: 7/7. When your numbers line up, things change.

Being alone in a bedsit in Chalk Farm was very conducive to my hermit-like tendencies. I knew very little about myself then, as I journeyed from one situation to another, trying to work out what life was all about, but the independence and sense of freedom I felt at that time was wonderful, if a little scary. The following year, the third 8 Personal Year in my life involved my first financial lessons, and I found myself in debt. My salary was £700 p.a. and living in London was not cheap. Cornflakes became a staple meal at dinner time on many occasions. I loved to buy clothes and most of my salary was spent on the pleasures of consumables. I had not yet learnt the lessons of financial prudence. Luckily, my father, once I had drummed up the courage to tell him, bailed me out, and I returned home and went to work as a temporary secretary, back on the trading estate.

I married my first husband at the age of 20, having met him on his return from Voluntary Service Overseas through the Missionary Society. I unknowingly trapped myself; I was financially secure, but trapped. I had barely stepped onto my stage. I knew little of my character, and certainly didn't understand that I could in fact write my own script. I thought getting married was the script. It was what my friends had done. I had been taught to iron shirts, cook, plan a cleaning regime, and so I fell in line. As I stood at the entrance to the church I knew that I was doing the wrong thing, but there was no going back. There were too many people to let down. Unfortunately letting myself down was at the bottom of the list. The date was the 7th July 1973, 7/7. Things changed.

Florence Campbell writing in *Your Days are Numbered* gives me comfort that my journey through 2018 was as it should be, and the enlightenment gained through material loss was all part of my journey.

The number 7 *'must not concern yourself with the accumulation of material possessions and must learn that he who loses his life (materially) shall find it (spiritually). You must apply spiritual laws to material affairs. Must rest, study, meditate, and be silent and know yourself. Must not insist upon partnerships or leadership. Must learn to understand the unseen world'*.

I will never know my father's insights into such things, but I do know that he loved to sit and ponder. He kept his thoughts to himself, and I often wonder how different things would have been if he had made his fortune. Would he have been happier? Who knows? Some 8s master the energy and make millions, and some, like my father, work hard and simply succeed in providing for their family, a noble thing. I know he made a difference to the people he came in contact with, dishing out a little bit of wisdom here and there, and my memory of him is always sitting in his favourite chair by the fire, with a thoughtful look on his face. I still wonder at the irony of the loss of money for both of us, especially given that mine was lost whilst residing in Ascot, the home of racing and a place that he loved dearly.

I reach the end of my 8 year, a little bit older, poorer, but richer, and a whole lot wiser. My diary once again sees me writing lists and reflecting, as I move towards the final year of my Epicycle.

DIARY ENTRY
13ᵗʰ DECEMBER, 2008 – ASCOT

The past year has been challenging to say the least, but…

· *Trelawney is finished*
· *The studio is finished and rented*
· *I have a new opportunity to run a course at Charters School*
· *The new literature is done*
· *The new business at Ascot Heath has gone well*
· *We have put on a successful*

> *Talent Show*
> *Adult Quiz*
> *Charity Quiz*
> *Seaside Special*
> *Xmas Quiz*

· *I have supportive neighbours*
· *The Right To Manage process is under way.*

What do I need to achieve in 2009?

· *Increase income through Right Livelihood*
· *Expand Numerology parties*
· *Rent somewhere by the sea*
· *Sing more, dance more, live more, love more*
· *Make a success of the FASBAT Cafe*
· *Sell Burleigh Wood House*

DIARY ENTRY
31st DECEMBER, 2008 – ASCOT

Sitting in FEGO's, my favourite cafe on the brink of 2009 is a sobering experience. I'm not sure I've achieved everything that was possible this year, in spite of my Overalls of Organisation and Suit of Success, but I don't seem to have stopped for a minute, and the achievements and failures are there to see and can be ticked off.

My confidence in myself is not yet absolute, and therefore I believe I am still a long way from realising my potential. This year has been a turning point, and I am becoming more and more aware that in order to reach my potential I will need to make some major changes. But things take time. It is five years since I sat in Malta dreaming up possibilities. There really are no shortcuts, especially when you wander from the path... but then had I not wandered from the path, I wouldn't know what I know now.

Goodbye 8 year see you next time around.

YEAR 9:

THE HUMANITARIAN

Keywords: Completion · Forgiveness · Transition

Underbalanced	**Right Action**	**Overbalanced**
indifferent		*intolerant*
uncaring		*self-centred*
unconcerned	SELFLESSNESS	*unreasonable*
inflexible	TOLERANCE	*greedy*
un-cooperative	GENEROSITY	*despondent*
distant	SYMPATHY	*over-emotional*
	COMPLETION	
	COMPASSION	
	RELEASE	

BE WILLING TO LET GO OF THE OLD AND UNDERSIRABLE

CHARACTER BRIEF
Humanitarian looking for cause

Costume	Props
Fleece of Forgiveness	Barrel of Benevolence
Unconditional Underwear	Cartload of Care
Transitional Tank-top	Large Bin

■ 9999999999999999999999 ■

YEAR 9: PARTING IS
SUCH SWEET SORROW

The 9 Personal Year brings you to the end of a complete nine-year cycle of your life. It is a year to complete unfinished business, reach conclusions and tie up loose ends. These actions will help you step into the next nine years of your life, without the pressure of unresolved matters of the past pulling you back.

Christine Delorey
Creative Numerology

If you have started reading this book in a 9 Personal Year, you may be relieved to know that endings are part of the vibration of the year. You may have been busily sorting out your wardrobe, whilst muttering to yourself about a whole 'new you', or if you moved house last year in your 8 year, you may have stumbled across a box in the loft, and wondered why on earth you couldn't manage to throw it out before you moved. Sadly you may have lost a loved one, or favourite pet, or you may find yourself with the urge to finish things which may have been hanging around for years; like a book you are writing, or a jumper you are knitting for a favourite relative. You may get married and tie the knot after a period of engagement, give birth, or come to the end of a contract you have been working on. Some things you will be very happy to rid yourself of, like the accumulated rubbish which has been collecting in the corner of the garage, but some things you will find harder like the loss of a friend, the death of a loved one, a move from a property, or the resolution of accumulated emotional baggage.

Letting go is probably one of the most challenging aspects of the 9 year. Even if change is needed, wanted, desired, and passionately entered into, it can still be difficult. But everything changes, nothing stays the same, people come, people go. Circumstances present themselves with unseen endings, forcing us to move on, move forward, grow. We do this on a daily basis, the minutiae going unnoticed. We flow in and out, good to bad, bad to good, navigating our way over, and around everything that seems to come to us and go from us. But in a 9 Personal Year, letting go can be a significant part of our personal growth.

I knew without a shadow of a doubt when entering my 9 year that things had to change big time, and the first thing to go was my worn out relationship. Having stuck to a much better understanding of what worked for me thanks to my consistent efforts at self-improvement, I knew that this was not for me. Thankfully, it ended amicably, leaving the friendship intact, a friendship which endures to this day. We hear and ignore the voice in our heads and hearts so many times, and we choose to ignore it at our peril. I had clung on to the idea of the relationship, even though the reality was that it had tremendous power to take me away from my dreams. But I was getting a taste for personal power, and I liked it. I had managed to hang on to everything I had learnt about myself throughout the relationship; what I did want, what I didn't want, and I had kept on a route which had seen me refusing to compromise, or co-operate with anything that did not sit right with me. May in a 9 year is a 5 month; a month which indicates movement progress and change. It is a busy and emotional month for me, but one which brings freedom due to the sale of my rental property. As predicted it is sold at a loss, but I had come to terms with the lesson learnt during my 8 Personal Year, and I am very happy to see the whole adventure concluded. I had gladly sold it to the family who had rented it from me, and they were delighted. This coincides with my daughter reaching the age of 18, and the cessation of my maintenance payments. I had dreaded this moment, but when it came, I was extremely happy to take a further step into my independence. It was a surprisingly empowering ending. But the item at the top of list of things I needed to leave my life, was still there; Burleigh Wood House. The difficulties involved in getting to the stage where this could happen, had hopefully been ironed out, and although there was no absolute resolution on the Right to Manage Company, I took a large breath and once again called in the estate agents.

I spend time in Wandsworth Common in August, house-sitting for my goddaughter. Trips on the 319 bus past Battersea and onto Sloane Square, take my mind away from any further endings that my 9 year might have in store for me. I am tempted by the windows filled with end of sale consumables, but know that a 9 Personal Year is all about getting rid of things, not buying new ones. I visit the British Museum and Camden Market, and meet up with my cousin and his wife, who I haven't seen for many years. My pregnant daughter-in-law visits, and we go to see *All's Well That Ends Well* at the National Theatre. Whilst away I receive some good news, although I try not to get too excited.

DIARY ENTRY
FRIDAY 14th AUGUST, 2009 – (8 MONTH, 4 DAY) – LONDON

Philip called regarding another viewing on the flat. Another mother and daughter. Hope the daughter likes Sophie's room. I hope that the place smells OK.

This leaves me hopeful that maybe at last, all will indeed end well, and I pray for a flourish of Shakespearian resolution.

On my return home I receive another phone call.

DIARY ENTRY
24th AUGUST, 2009 – (8 MONTH, 5 DAY) – ASCOT

Talk about go with the flow....

The flat is allegedly sold, and the Lands Tribunal has refused leave to appeal. My difficult neighbour had appealed causing delay after delay. My upstairs neighbour, Denise is really fed up with me for selling the flat. I have no fridge; it has decided to give up the ghost, not an ending I was after quite yet, and it is a real pain ... how ridiculous ... everything has changed and I feel rather wobbly.

It is an 8 month in my 9 year. Of course it is. It is a month for contracts, money, solicitors, agreements. I never thought I would see the day, as there had been so many obstacles to surmount but finally, after more difficult phone calls to the Lands Tribunal, and expensive calls to my solicitor, the Right to Manage is administered and the sale is on the table. In my desire to leave the property and garden in a better state than I found it, I find myself frantically cleaning and sorting out what is to remain in my life, and what is to go.

My 9 year was giving me a real opportunity to have a sort out and tie up loose ends. The end of my maintenance payments, and my daughter's 'coming of age' had allowed me to reflect on the disconnection from my marriage. It felt as if the binding had been loosened. But there was still a little wriggling and forgiveness needed to free myself completely, but at least the practical and legal ending was to be a steppingstone to my future independence.

The advice in the 9 year is to let things that are trying to leave your life leave, unhindered, without you standing in the way, trying to hang on to things that have gone past their sell by date. The 9 year also brings with it the opportunity to go deep into our emotional centre, and change how we feel about things which are keeping us stuck in the past; to forgive self, and real or imagined foes, and to discard anything and everything that is holding us back. Forgiveness is key. Holding onto pain, or anger, or bitterness is completely detrimental to any sense of wellbeing or flow. It causes stasis. In the end it is a simple choice. The choice is ours to make. You either choose to forgive or you don't. When you choose not to forgive it's as if you are holding your breath, and all the time you choose to do this you stop the flow; the flow between you and other people, you yourself, and life in general. Peace is the end result of the 9 year, when you allow yourself to jettison any weight you have carried. This Right Action puts you in a much better position to approach the next cycle with a feeling of renewal and lightness.

During the process of clearing away my clutter, my childhood memories take me back to Hartlepool and the Park Hotel, owned by Uncle Tommy and Auntie Edna; I used to lay awake at night and wonder at the commotion coming through the ceiling. It sounded so romantic. People talking, music playing on the juke box, doors opening and closing, laughter. Being a terribly curious Gemini, I wanted to be down there in the hub of things. I couldn't quite hear the conversations, but the snippets I did hear turned into adventures in my head, and just like Robert Louis Stevenson in his poem *My Bed is a Boat*, I sailed away into the night till I could hear no more, returning in the morning to the safety of my room. The people who frequented Uncle Tommy's watering hole were a colourful bunch, and as I lay there I would imagine that all of life's difficulties would be taken to the pub to be drowned in beer. Broken parts of conversations, raised voices, laughter and tears all seeped through the ceiling and into my consciousness as I drifted off into another world.

In the morning, I was allowed down into the bars, where the quiet emptiness brushed away the mysterious ideas and imaginings of the previous night. The framework of the illusion still remained, as I walked through the large heavy doors into what I then thought was heaven. I was allowed to clean the tables and collect the bar towels for washing. They were still soaking wet from the previous night's activity, and the smell of the bar stays with me to this day. One of my favourite jobs was gathering up all of the beer mats from the tables, and sorting them into un-used, used, slightly used, and no longer of any use. I would build towers from them, constructing a box of four with a diagonal mat on top on which to build another layer. This was a tricky operation which completely held my attention. It took me a while to work out that if you use the mats that have been soaked in beer and have become distorted, then they make it much harder to construct the tower. I tried and tried to make them all work, especially when I didn't have enough, but in the end had to listen to Uncle Tommy's instructions, and throw away the mats which were no longer of any use.

One of my favourite poems is by T.S. Eliot, 'The Four Quartets', and the last poem in the quartet entitled 'Little Gidding' has always resonated with me. Elliot speaks of endings and beginnings, epitaphs, and apple trees.

What we call the beginning is often the end.
And to make an end is to make a beginning.
The end is where we start from.

I knew in my heart that there were to be endings. I didn't need my newfound numerological knowledge telling me I was in a 9 year, and at the end of a cycle, I just knew. My daughter was 18, and the piano had long gone, freeing me from the bindings that it had placed around me. A new imagining had been found on my travels, and I had decided that I had no choice but to develop my work further. I had tried to ignore it, but it was like a piece of Sellotape stuck to my finger that just wouldn't come off. I knew for certain that the stress of my financial situation had to end, and that meant the sale of my flat and my rental property. My relationship was over, and I was running out of ideas and enthusiasm for FASBAT.

They say you shouldn't start anything new in a 9 year, you should merely clear space for what is to come. I had pushed myself towards expansion in my 8 year, clutching at any straw I could to make more money, and I had secured some business at a local school which was to start in the January. It wasn't at all what I wanted to do, but I seemed to be stuck on the train tracks of trying to make money through any means possible. Luckily, the universe stepped in and the course was cancelled due to lack of funds. This was one of the first things to go in my 9 year. It had seemed extremely important in my 8 year, but the relief was monumental. I put the phone down and burst into tears. This was accompanied by sobbing. This hasn't happened very often in my life, but when it has it has felt like a huge lump of emotion which has been stuck within me, has been pushed to the surface. It lays me bare for a day, but when I recover from the unexpected outburst I feel a renewal as if an enormous weight has been lifted. For me, strong emotional outpourings are difficult things to deal with, and I therefore suppress a lot of emotion. This I have learnt is not a healthy thing to do. Better out than in has become my experience, and I have become better at it; more aware of an emotion rising within me, and more willing to feel the pain in order to release myself. To successfully navigate the 9 year you need to have the courage to go to places you would much rather deny, due to the possibility of emotional pain. You may get resistance from friends and family, who are not on the same page as you, and it will feel easier to stay in the dressing room rather than stand in the spotlight, and face the reaction of an audience who don't like the way the play is going.

Things can pop up in a 9 year from your past in order to effect some kind of resolution. Synchronicity is everywhere if you care to stay resolutely in the present, with awareness. On the very day I am writing about my release from a 9 year Epicycle in September 2018, a 9 month in a 9 year, an Epicycle further on from my diaries, I receive a phone call from my old neighbours. I haven't been in contact with them for many many years and there they are calling me and wanting to meet up. Did all the energy in the Universe dance around and leap from my thoughts to their thoughts and memories. Why are they visiting the place where I now live, at that very particular moment in the time continuum? I have no idea, and I smile in the knowledge that really, we know nothing. It is a mystery. I can't explain how things just tie up; they just do.

I tell them that I have just been writing about them in my book, and they too are struck by the coincidence. We talk about the happy times, the difficult times and the moving on times. I am apparently forgiven for moving away and leaving them to face the rest of the music alone. If you need to move away from friends or family in a 9 year for whatever reason, and they were very upset with me leaving them behind, you can be assured that if that friendship is genuine and that bonds have been forged from love and compatible values, then that friendship will still be there the other side of any metamorphosis you are undergoing.

October sees me sitting in the garden on my favourite bench, looking at what I had created with my bare hands, and once again I sob my heart out. I had to keep remembering a phrase I had picked up from some self-help book somewhere 'just let the pain run through you; don't fight it'. I knew it was time for me to leave, but so much of me didn't want to. I guess I felt like a failure. I had lost a lot of money in my 8 year and that didn't feel good, but in a strange way it didn't feel so bad either; it had given me the leverage I needed to move on. Had I made a profit and gone on to invest in another property, I may well have stayed. But the time was right, although I was very nervous that a trapdoor would open, the sale would fall through, and I would be back to square one.

One of the features in the 9 year would appear to be the abundance of dreams. Dreams seem to have the most amazing ability to work things out for you. Our subconscious is a very powerful and wonderful thing, and I find it stepping in to help out with the clearing process. Intent seems to be all that is needed, although I have found with some things, that no matter how much I want to move on from them, they just refuse to go. A bit like my flat, which obviously was not going to let me go until I had learned the lesson of Independence. 1, Burleigh Wood House clearly had its own timetable.

A dream which is documented during this particular period, had immense power. It came like the wind, and then disappeared back into the unknown.

DIARY ENTRY
12th SEPTEMBER, 2009 – (9 YEAR, 9 MONTH, 3 DAY) – ASCOT

Woke up this morning feeling emotionally exhausted. Slipped in and out of consciousness and took myself through the forest in my head, to the place where I felt myself surrounded by a deep blue colour. Steps led me down into an underground cavern with five coffins. Each of the coffins contained things from my past, which had kept me rooted and unable to truly move forward.

· Childhood/mother
· 1st husband, 2nd husband, 3rd husband
· Burleigh Wood House

I buried each of the coffins and said goodbye to everything. The work was surprisingly easy, but slow. As I worked my way through the digging and the burying, I felt myself becoming stronger and stronger. Each coffin contained all of the emotions and difficulties surrounding their place in my life. The joys and reasons to be grateful were placed in a basket next to a large oak tree. When the job was done, I picked up the basket and walked back up the steps and into the forest. The entrance was sealed. As I walked away I became bathed in a silver light which shimmered and sent arrows out into the dense forest, lighting my way back to consciousness.

Earlier in the year in July, my 7 personal month I had spent time away in deep contemplation working through my relationship conundrums, trying to understand why I had been so unsuccessful in my connection to others.

DIARY ENTRY
22nd JULY, 2009 – (9 YEAR, 7 MONTH) – ASCOT

I am in fact lonely – not something that I care to admit to, but it is the truth. I am at a crossroads and I have a vague idea of which road to take, but I have many unanswered questions.

I am, it would seem, concerned with giving love, and getting it. But it seems to be the thing I keep failing at. WHY?

When I had married my first husband I was 20 years of age. I met him whilst working in London. I knew very little of myself. I saw my friends getting married, and despite the freedom and adventure I had found away from my hometown, I did what I thought was right. I got married and took up my position making omelettes, ironing serviettes, and trying to fulfil his mother's idea of the perfect wife.

Looking at my relationships through the lens of astrology and numerology, gave me a form of understanding which I needed to enable me to move forward. It showed missmatched energies both astrologically and from a numerological perspective. A Gemini/Taurus rub, a 6/7 rub, and fire/air rub. Importantly there was also in every case a mismatch of values, combined with my acting out of a different character in each marriage to try and make it fit.

When some people 'fail' at relationship, they remain stuck and never move on, becoming bitter and unable to forgive. This wasn't an option for me. I have always been driven by the need to understand and find the truth in things, and this is a large part of who I am. It seems rather flaky to say that my understanding of astrology and numerology helped me to finally move on, but I take comfort from the words of Matthew Goodwin writing in the forward of his book *Numerology – The Complete Guide: 'Why does numerology work? There are many explanations in literature – discussions of psychic energy, the God force, the vibratory effect of numbers. These explanations have not clarified anything for me. Frankly, I don't know why numerology works. I don't know whether the numbers are merely a descriptive code or representation of a force determining people's behaviour. Numerology, like other occult fields, does not, at this time, allow for scientific explanation. I can only attest to the fact, confirmed by other numerologists and their clients, of the consistent congruence between a person's numbers and that person's characteristics and life experience.'*

My analysis of past relationship shows that it is not enough just to look at the astrology a person has. I generally just look to the Sun Signs for a guide and what I find most interesting is the elemental analysis. The idea of an air sign fanning the flames of a fire sign always makes me smile. I know exactly the hot air produced by three air signs, in the same room at the same time, and I have also observed two water signs drowning each other, or a fire sign reducing a water sign to a puddle. But until I add the numerology of the person into the analysis, I only have half of the picture.

Looking at my relationship analysis, I can see that the energies involved caused immense difficulties. Numbers rubbing against each other causing the most problems. Of course this isn't to say that someone else with more knowledge, or a different set of numbers or different upbringing, level of support, etc. could have made the relationships work. Sadly, I couldn't; I didn't have the wisdom. It may seem wrong to have drawn comfort from cold analysis, but I did. All the emotion and pain still lay underneath needing release, but for me in my 9 Personal Year in my 5th Epicycle, through analysis and a desire to find the truth, I managed to bury and put to rest left over elements of my past. Any residual pain evaporated. The 9 year is an opportunity to peel away any masks we have created, and to consider the possibilities of a script re-write. Sometimes, the script may just need a little tweaking, sometimes you may want to throw it away and start again. Understanding your partners' numerology, and in particular what Personal Year they are in, can help tremendously in understanding the different energies at play, enabling co-operation and harmonisation. So with the dreams behind me and many things concluded and resolved it is almost time to move on.

Contracts are exchanged and the process of packing begins. The furniture I had accumulated during my time at Burleigh Wood House was rather large. Many happy hours had been spent at the Ascot Racecourse Auction, buying things to fill the lofty and elegant dwelling, but sadly they too had to go. A good friend had offered me a place to rent in the annexe attached to her house. It was perfect. The first time I saw it, during the first year of our time spent at university together in 1998, I said out loud, 'I love this; I want to live here'. Little did I know that I had set in motion something which would manifest itself at exactly the right time. She had offered it to me at the start of the year, knowing that I wanted to try and sell the flat. I held the possibility in my thoughts, and in spite of being rented out to someone else in the meantime, it became available just when I needed it, and I was very happy to take her up on her offer. I went through everything I possessed and contemplated its place in my life. Many things went, but I hung on to anything I absolutely loved. Furniture went to family and friends, apart from a few pieces which I took with me. Clothes were taken to the charity shop, and a car boot sale saw the departure of a collection of knicks knacks and assorted items, which no longer had a place in my heart.

A farewell party on 22nd October, a 1 month of new beginnings in my 9 year, saw a wonderful collection of family, friends and neighbours come together, to remember the good times at Burleigh Wood, and to celebrate my new start. There were songs, poems, stories, and much merriment as they helped me to say goodbye to this particular chapter. The sorrow turned into sweetness, and by the time I closed the door I was ready for the next chapter. The 1 energy contained in my Number 1 flat had helped me grow towards independence, and the 9 energy had helped me to say goodbye, knowing that I had resolved past issues, left the flat better than I had found it, and in the hands of a legally formed Right to Manage Company, that would enable the new owner to live there, with control over her surroundings. And so a whole Epicycle concluded. I have no idea what to expect in the next one except the unexpected.

YEAR 1:

THE PIONEER

Keywords: New Beginnings · Courage · Independence

Underbalanced	**Right Action**	*Overbalanced*
defeatist		*arrogant*
dependent		*headstrong*
passive	BOLDNESS	*rigid*
insecure	ACTIVITY	*greedy*
fearful	CREATIVITY	*selfish*
submissive	DYNAMISM	*stubborn*
	ASPIRATION	
	PROGRESSION	

EXPECT THE UNEXPECTED

CHARACTER BRIEF
Bold adventurer looking for something new

Costume	Props
Cloak of Courage	Sword of Strong Will
Pioneering Pants	Sandwiches
Dinner Jacket	Independent Spirit

■ 11111111111111111111 ■

YEAR 1:

RIGHT BUS – WRONG WAY

Be ready for MAJOR CHANGES. You will be inspired to start new projects or enterprises. You will feel a strong push towards new goals. This is a year of opportunities. Be open minded, organised, and focused. Avoid distractions and procrastinations. There are many changes you must make, and much work to be done.

Hans Decoz
Numerology

Unusually there is just one entry in my diary for January in my 1 Personal Year. But it was a 2 month, a month for rest and harmony, and I was under the covers after possibly the strangest Christmas of my life.

Having moved into my friend's apartment post sale, I spent a lot of time making it feel like home, a task I had greatly enjoyed. I was just starting to feel my roots settle down into my new surroundings, when I had to move out over Christmas due to a family wedding. The wedding was on Christmas Eve and was a beautiful affair. The snow fell just in the nick of time, turning it into something approaching a fairy tale.

Afterwards, I headed for my son's house to spend the night and join them for Christmas lunch. It was good to be with family, especially as it was my grandchild's first Christmas, and it was filled with love and cuddles. But it felt as if my new tender roots had been ripped out of the ground, leaving me feeling decidedly wobbly. For the first time in my life I felt homeless. I move back to Highfields just after Christmas and retreat. The house has no number, but the name equates to a number 7. I felt very at home in the energy, and was grateful for such a lovely cave in which to rest my head.

DIARY ENTRY
6th JANUARY, 2010 – BRAY

I am feeling rather down, and I have a worrying feeling that I am exhausting the people who surround me. My son has rung me to ask if I am ok. This does not happen. I must be bad. My body is screaming at me and the menopause is insisting that I take a different approach. I feel rather stuck. Here I am in January, which can seem like the cruellest month, in spite of the fact that T.S. Elliot says it is April. It isn't; it's January 2010. I feel as if I am in my very own version of his poem the 'Wasteland' and go to ground like a wounded dog seeking respite.

I decided to give myself permission to rest, and relaxed into the new energy. The 2 energy is a slow energy and requires that you wait, be patient and stay in the background. Giving ourselves permission is such an empowering feeling. So often we deny ourselves what we need; there is the worry about what people might think. They may think we're lazy, they might think we have no backbone, or that we are being selfish; but I didn't want to go anywhere. I drag myself back to work, and immediately come home and get back under the duvet. Our body tells us all the time what it needs, but we become deaf or tune out. It can be very strange when you enter a whole new Epicycle, as the overall push is towards new beginnings, but it is important that we take the time to rest, so that we can harness our strength, in order to make the most of the opportunities that may leap out at us in a 1 year. It is a time to look through the seed catalogue, and if you have put in the work of weeding out the unnecessary debris in your 9 year, then you will be ready for action when the time is right.

When I re-emerge in February I start to feel like creating a plan. I am in a 3 month, and I am hoping something magic will jump onto the page. I visited a friend at St Mary's Hospital London, and left feeling that I needed to work harder to address my health, or lack of it. Seeing someone who hasn't listened to the warning signs, and has ended up severely challenged and debilitated by the physical side of our existence, is a sure fire way to focus the mind on what we need to change. I had popped into the British Library for the first time before the visit, and was deeply moved by the leather-bound handrail which seemed to speak volumes to me. I look up at the books and feel a stirring within my soul and an urge to carry on writing.

On my return, I head for the diary I had purchased just before Christmas, in anticipation of inspiration, and I was keen to make the most of it and record everything. It had a very loud and colourful pink cover with the word 'POW!' in large white letters. But I wasn't quite ready for that level of energy, so put it to one side and spend a lovely couple of hours wandering around the shops, looking for something more suitable. A plain orange journal jumps out at me and is purchased, along with a cup of coffee and time to reflect.

FIRST THINGS FIRST

There is an exercise I use in workshops which I call the 'Circle of Life'. It is a good way of identifying which area of your life could do with some attention. The depths of January are always a great time to take time off, on your own, or with your partner, to consider what the forthcoming year might hold in terms of dreams and aspirations. Talking about ideas and batting around strategies with friends or family, might not be everyone's idea of fun; you may wish to keep things to yourself, but it always leads to understanding of the other characters on your stage, and shared experiences can help to clarify uncertainties, acting as inspiration in the search for personal growth.

The Health section of my circle, which contained such things as Career, Environment, Finance, Personal Development, Fun and Recreation, Significant Other, Spirituality, and Friends threw up the lowest score at the start of 2010. I wasn't exactly treating my body like a temple. There was no regular exercise, and I certainly wasn't eating properly. There was to be no journey forward until a few things had been addressed. With the sale of my flat, my financial sector which last January had been at a very low ebb, had risen significantly. I had money in the bank, a salary coming in, and thanks to the interest rate, a very nice sum of money each month. This more than paid for my accommodation and expenses, and I felt very blessed. But my career section was troubling me. I was working hard, and the business was successful, and I had been making inroads into developing my Personal Philosophy Programme, but the words mission, vision, and purpose weren't drawn up clearly enough in my mind. I drew a line across the middle of the section and scored it a five, as I continued the exercise, my wheel started to look very uneven and lacking in balance. I decided to start with the lowest number and make a plan to get some exercise.

I start by walking around the village each day. I set small achievable goals, and was pleased to have something positive to focus on. I didn't know what the year was going to throw at me, and my pioneering pants were feeling a little tight.

DIARY ENTRY
SUNDAY 21st FEBRUARY, 2010 - BRAY

It has been a rather good day today, placed in the context of the last two months, which have been rather challenging. The walk around the village this morning was very enjoyable, although I was disappointed at not being able to gain entry to Bray Church, so I sat outside and meditated, amongst the souls who had already been through the process of living, and found themselves on the other side. In spite of my bones hurting I felt good after the walk. I must keep it up as I am starting to feel alive again and ready for action.

I continue with the regime, which might not seem like very much, but it doesn't take much, just consistency, and I soon start to feel my energy levels rising. March sees the weather brightening up, along with my spirit, and I spend happy times with friends, family, and work colleagues. The weight that I had removed from my shoulders in my 9 year, was starting to pay dividends. My money was safely in the bank, and I no longer had the stress of Burleigh Wood House hanging over me. Work was very busy with several shows planned and all of a sudden, my business partner was surging forward with new ideas for expansion. She had never been to the Edinburgh Fringe, and I suggest we take a trip later in the year for the purposes of inspiration.

As I make my way through the year I try to find somewhere else to live. I really have no idea where I want to be, making it a very arduous and confusing task. Despite the fact that I have moved on and stand on the edge of new beginning, my dreams of a new life on a small island in New Zealand seemed to have dissipated, and nothing seems right, but I carry on looking. Renting from a friend is great. We have each other for company and enjoy rattling around together, and I have come to regard it as my second home, but I know it's only temporary.

At the end of March I have an overwhelming desire to celebrate spring, and arrange to have a party. Towards the end of my 9 year I had been reacquainted with some long standing theatrical friends. We had come together to celebrate the life of a much loved fellow thespian, who had died from a heart attack. We had all performed in a musical show called 'Godspell' in 1984 and on hearing of the loss, the director of the show had contacted a few people and asked if they would like to get together to celebrate our friend's life with a concert production.

Our children and his, had all grown up, and many of them took part in the concert, which included numbers from the original show, along with excerpts from other shows close to his heart. In a year of endings when I was moving on from so much of my past, it was wonderful to reconnect with people who were at the centre of my passion for musical theatre. And so, I invite old friends, new friends, work colleagues, and family into my new year to celebrate Spring and the promise that it held.

Still looking for a big change I take a trip to the coast with my eldest daughter. I have a mad idea that I could rent somewhere for work, and maybe have a place by the sea for weekends. New Zealand had slipped away, due the distance involved and the looks on the faces of my children, but there was something about my desire to be by the sea that remained close to my heart. We stay at a seaside town on the South Coast, and she asks me if this is where I have chosen to come and die. This was not my plan; I had stuff to do – but I took her point. I remind her of how I had fallen in love with Waiheke Island in New Zealand and the draw of the sea. We drink coffee, walk, laugh and put Eastbourne to bed, despite its seaside loveliness.

The 1 year energy suggests that we should expect the unexpected, and as I travel through the year trying to make things happen, I leave no room for the unexpected. I am trying to drive the Universe forward, instead of going about my daily business, putting my energy into the things that are currently in front of me, whilst listening with two ears. I try to buy a house closer to where the business is. I almost put a deposit down, but I know it's just not right as it would be a complete compromise. But I was keen to re-accommodate my daughter who had decided right at the last moment, not to go to university, not to live with her father, and not to live with me in Bray. She was determined to stay in Ascot, and had rented a room close to where she had taken a job. I pulled out and trusted my instinct, that this wasn't the big change I was looking for. I felt strangely empowered by this decision, and wondered if I might at last be listening to my instinct, with two ears.

Whilst sat in the garden on my favourite bench just before I left Ascot, I became very scared contemplating the future. To stop the shaking I drove over to Bray to reacquaint myself with where I was about to deposit myself. As I was driving Barry Manilow came on the radio singing at the top of his voice...

Something's comin' up
And I don't know what it is
Something's comin' up
And I don't know where it's gonna take me
But there's something dyin'
Something bein' born

The CD sits in the side pocket of my car, and I play the song over and over again. I remind myself to hold the dream of the sea, the programme, the writing, and to have faith that all would be well. Life carries on in what seems in a good direction, and I am taken along to a networking group by a friend, which, I take to like a duck to water. I spend several evenings in the following months, meeting new people in a very conducive setting, talking about my ideas. The meetings are full of people with dreams in their heart and the atmosphere is electric. Opportunities arise at every meeting, but I have the feeling that I am still stuck on the train tracks of the same old thing.

May sees my life full of duties, responsibility, and family birthdays. The addition of my first grandchild to the family in the previous December is a complete joy, and my family ties are strengthened. We all seem to want to be together more, and I can see how New Zealand would never have worked; the distance was just too great. But my feet were still itchy, and my desire for something new was growing day by day, the sea was still calling, and I took every opportunity to take a trip down to the coast.

June brings the culmination of the FASBAT shows which include a 10th Anniversary Show, a Circus Show, a Talent Show, and a Pantomime. My desire to make a difference was certainly in play, and the personal development seen in each and every child was, as usual, something to be applauded. But I was running out of ideas going forward, and for me this is never a good sign. I welcomed the summer with open arms, especially as the apartment I was renting was blessed with a swimming pool. July sees me expanding my fitness with daily swims and walks around the village, but I remain restless.

When one chapter finishes and another begins, there is a sense of excitement which carries you forward into the story of your life. Unknown twists and turns await and you can sometimes wander down roads, which for some reason, aren't on the map. These roads look so promising initially, enticing you with their mysterious, non-conformist direction. 'I wonder what's around the next corner' becomes the mantra of change, like a holiday destination yet to be explored, full of brochured promises, and as yet unknown delights. But there comes a time when the initial energy, that vital energy needed to effect change wanes, leaving a plateau. By the time I get to August, I have stopped trying to push my way into something new, and head north on my annual cultural pilgrimage.

Sitting on the top of a big red bus in Edinburgh ready to take on the Edinburgh Fringe, the realisation that 'I was on the right bus, but going in the wrong direction', pulled me up short. I needed to disembark, stand on the other side of the road and try again, but my need for caffeine overtook my need to get myself to my digs, unpack my bag and make myself at home, and so I placed myself in a seat in the nearest cafe with a window on the world. The desire to dump my life onto paper had been thwarted at the airport, and again on the plane. My late arrival to Terminal 4 left time only for a re-checking of my tickets, and a dash to buy some much needed inspiration in the bookstore. The Philosophy of Donkeys leaps off the shelf at me and into my already heavy bag. Maybe there are some words of wisdom contained within, which will allow the beast of burden to lighten my load, and take me in a different direction. So, complete with a full fat cappuccino and complimentary biscuit, a blank page in my diary, and a pen desperate to scribble cathartically, I brace myself for a much needed revelation. Nothing. The caffeine kicks in, the sugar kicks in, the confusion kicks in. Nothing.

My life, despite its busyness felt like an old empty shed. Gone were the left over bits of wood, old paint tins, rusty nails, bits of string, and very dead spiders. No more holding myself together with things that had passed. The loss of everything I had left behind, had the power to leave me feeling so vulnerable that I could have crawled back under the duvet, and stayed there until the four horses of the apocalypse were heard on the gravelled drive. I was in limbo, that place between one thing and another. But luckily I had been in limbo before, and recognised its status as temporary.

So, safe in the knowledge that my money is securely deposited in the bank, supporting the very sensible decision not to compromise or do anything hastily, I make my way to the bus stop on the other side of the road, where there is a bus waiting to take me in the 'right direction'. My arrival for yet another year at the vacated student flat, is greeted by the familiar sticky carpets, brown furniture, and a nothingness normally welcomed by the hermit in me. After all, it is mad out there on Princes Street, and I am prone to a bit of leafy respite as provided by this southerly suburb. I would normally be sharing this high ceilinged, once elegant space, with friends keen to soak up the culture, engage in holiday banter, and down a few glasses of wine. But, unexpectedly, I am here on my own. My business partner's wrecked back is the culprit for my singularity, but the plane ticket was booked, and ideas were needed. I put the kettle on and try to devise a plan of action.

Shows to see, exhibitions to visit, friends to catch up with. But it is like pushing a boulder up a very steep hill; it just doesn't feel right, and proves more difficult than the Times crossword. But I have to push on. My business of ten years needs new input, and this is why I am here. To be inspired. Nothing.

The struggle continues through the uneventful evening's televisual entertainment, and follows me into bed. An itinerary, honed out of desperation, lies limply on the bedside table. Lights out. As my head hits the pillow the words 'right bus wrong way, right bus wrong way', provides a looped accompaniment to the unlit disco which has taken over my semi-conscious mind. I drift fitfully. I force myself awake and text a friend 'I'm in trouble, are you awake?' The phone rings, 'That's funny just got out of bed and picked up my guitar. I was playing 'Troubled Child' when your text came in. What's up'? We talk and talk and talk. The monster leaves the cupboard, and like a scene from a movie, I sit bolt upright. That's it. That's the one. The missing piece. I can't carry on with the business.

Simple.

My business is tying me to a place where I no longer belong. It needs to go, along with the paint and dead spiders. My friends 'don't be ridiculous' exclamation floats into one ear and straight out of the other one. Whoa – the big one. Sleep ... piece of cake.

Selling the flat had uprooted me and I was holding up my roots like a dance dress. This decision was correct, it felt right, it felt good and I felt at peace. The idea of giving up something I had built over ten years had been hanging around in my head for some time, but I had pushed it into the dark recesses, where it had been having a nap. My friends words morphed into my metaphorical monkey, and took its place on my shoulder, next to my right ear. But that was ridiculous, wasn't it? I couldn't be homeless and jobless could I? My friends and family join in forming a chorus in my mind, and throw all sorts of obstacles and objections at me. But that was it. It had to go, along with the rusty nail that was pinning me to the floor. I needed to stay on the bus, but I needed to go in a different direction. Sat at the railway station in Maidenhead less than 24 hours previously, I had been confronted with an enormous billboard stating, 'Sometimes Something Changes Everything'. My decision matched the enormity of the billboard and had me reaching for a blank sheet of paper to start writing a new plan. Nothing.

The next day I leave the flat without a map. By the time I have descended five flights of stairs and got to the end of the block, I decide this is wholly providential, and from now on I will play it by ear, go with the flow and follow my instinct. The call to inform my business partner of my decision passes without pain. Either of us could have made the call at any time. We had an unspoken agreement that, all would be well. And it was, and for this I am grateful. When I say I want to get away and do something entirely barmy like look after donkeys, I am pointed in the direction of her place of birth, the Isle of Wight.

And so decision made, I make my way home, with my new itinerary on the back of an envelope, re-pack my bags and head straight for the ferry, and the town of Ventnor. I have a vague recollection of having been here before, but can't quite pin it down. The hotel I have chosen is fabulous. I decided I could push the boat out for four days and treat myself to something a little more exciting than a standard B&B. The hotel is owned by a Danish man and the decor is soothing, simple, and extremely tasteful. I feel very pleased with myself. I have responded to the unexpected, and found myself with an enormous feeling of relief. There is an air here of New Zealand and I love it. It's a little like going back in time. There are rather a lot of hills and I find myself challenged by the walk down to the esplanade, in spite of my partly honed new body. The flat Berkshire countryside seems a million miles away. Luckily, there is a seat halfway down and as I sit down, my phone mysteriously manages to ring my now ex-business partner. Very strange. I take the phone out of my pocket and we chat. I am looking over Ventnor Bay and directly down upon a business owned by her ex-dancing partner. She had told me the story of how, just as they were about to embark on a dancing tour of Europe, she had met and fallen in love with her now husband. She had, just like me decided not to carry on, but to take a different path. It was as if karma had closed the circle. I love when you are confronted with signs. For me they can be visual, like the billboard, or physical, like the flash of knowingness to my brain, or verbal in the form of a story. I particularly love it when I am thinking about something, and spot a white feather. I take these things to assure myself that I am on the right path.

As I sit and look at the sun shining on the sea, I start to formulate a plan to rent somewhere over the winter months, in an attempt to write a book based on my diaries. I find the nearest rental agent and arrange to see a cottage. It's really the only option and not to my taste, but as the owner tells me about the beauty of the moon shining on the sea, I fall in love with the romanticism, and sign on the dotted line. For some reason I don't hesitate for a second. It's September and I am in a 1 month in a 1 year. I have my pioneering pants at the ready, which now fit a little better due to my walking regime, and my cloak of courage is firmly wrapped around me. My independent spirit is flowing through me and I feel amazing. I was ready for something to change everything. Bring it on. I had no doubt in my mind that the road ahead would contain twists and turns, but my heart knew that this was the 'something'. I didn't know how, I just knew. As I stood on the edge of a new beginning all of the difficulties of the past nine years fell away.

I would need my sword of strong will, as I made my way back to break the news to family and friends, and I was ready for resistance. It's not that the people closest to you don't want you to be happy, when you make a monumental life-changing decision. But there are many reasons, none of which will have anything to do with you, why strong reactions bubble up to the surface, when people are faced with change. My children were all grown up and independent, but I still had to wrestle with feelings of guilt. I had struggled all my life with the idea of abandonment, and I wouldn't wish those feelings on anyone. But I had come to realise that we are not abandoned, we abandon ourselves. Abandoning my dreams of a different life for myself would, in the long run, be far worse than staying in a place and situation where my life force diminished.

The 1 year is about self; it is a year to be self-centred or, and its sounds much better when you say it like this, 'centred in self'. Independence is key and this can only be gained through self-referral; self-centred, self-referral. Sounds really bad doesn't it. But consider the alternative.

A passage from a book *A Return to Love* by Marianne Williamson had been rolling around in my head throughout my transition. It visited me again as I stood looking at the donkeys on my way back to the ferry. I find the passage deeply reassuring, and as I look at my new furry friends, who had mostly been rescued from circumstances beyond their control, I retrace my steps to this point in my life.

'...Our deepest fear is not that we are inadequate.
Our deepest fear is that we are powerful beyond measure.
It is our light, not our darkness that most frightens us.
We ask ourselves, who am I to be brilliant, gorgeous, talented, fabulous?
Actually, who are you not to be?
You are a child of God.
Your playing small does not serve the world.
There is nothing enlightened about shrinking so that other people won't feel insecure around you.

We are all meant to shine, as children do.
We were born to make manifest the glory of God that is within us.
It's not just in some of us; it's in everyone.

And as we let our own light shine, we unconsciously give other people permission to do the same.
As we are liberated from our own fear, our presence automatically liberates others.'

This little light of mine is the song of choice on the way back to the ferry terminal, and I leave the island feeling excited and full of hope for my future.

On my return I am faced with open mouths, stunned silences, and comments like 'the Isle of Wight ... it's sinking surely?' and 'I bet they don't have department stores'. Yes, I reply but they do have donkeys, and the sea, and frankly I need a complete change. I want to write a book on Numerology, so I have rented somewhere for six months. More silent remarks.

I put what remains of my life in storage, and just take a few of my most treasured possessions. My diaries, my books, some photos, and a few random objet d'art. My eldest daughter comes with me, and despite her reservations, helps me to move into the cottage. I'm not sure she can really believe her eyes, but I tell her about the moon on the water, and hope she doesn't think I have completely lost the plot. A print of the hands at the centre of the Sistine Chapel Fresco, which shows God and Adam almost touching is hung on the wall, and immediately smashes onto the floor. It feels like a bad omen, and I wonder if my desire and reality will ever come together and touch. Everything felt so near, and yet so far. The hands now sit happily in separate frames adorning my wall (securley hung), and I now know that the gap between our dreams and reality is the place where life is. A place where ideas exist, and where everything changes, a place at the top of our breath where anything is possible. Breathe in ... there it is ... breathe out.

My daughter leaves to catch the ferry, to return the van that has brought me to my destination. I hide my tears as she leaves, and as I close the door I wonder, just for a split second if I have done the right thing. After a week I am completely in love. The moon on the water during the first full moon fills me with wonder. It shines down upon the sea like a spotlight, and I just can't take my eyes off it. I am transported back to New Zealand, and I am mesmerised. I am so much closer to all the people that I love and in spite of the fear, which visits me from time to time I knew for sure that I had made the right decision.

Waiheke Island had been a signpost to something I couldn't really articulate, but something had been set in motion by my innermost desires, and here I was settling down to type up my diaries. They make me smile, laugh out loud, and cry. I consider everything I have learnt to date, and renew my desire to make a difference through the wisdom I have gained on my journey. As I look at the moon on the water, I remember that the circle is the Pythagorean symbol for the number 1 – the Monad, the symbol of new beginnings and I know that for now I am exactly where I need to be.

Talking to random strangers holds no fear for me, and I therefore quickly acquaint myself with the locals. I start looking for somewhere more permanent to live which takes me all over the island, but in the end all roads lead back to Ventnor, that quirky seaside town on an island loved by Dickens, Alfred Noyes, Lord Tennyson, Karl Marx, Queen Victoria, Longfellow, Winston Churchill, and many others. I feel in good company.

I purchase a small two-bedroom flat overlooking the most spectacular view and move in on 6th December, 2010. It is a 4 month in my 1 Personal Year. A month to put down roots, build a home and work towards stability. I am a little torn, as it is my granddaughter's 1st birthday and I am not there. But

I have called myself Grannie Grannie in honour of a dear friend's mother-in-law, who told me once that it was my duty to be 'unexpectedly interesting'. I hope that as my granddaughter grows older she will appreciate the sentiment, and forgive me for not being there for her 1st birthday.

My 1 Personal Year, the start of a whole new Epicycle, had certainly turned out to be unexpectedly interesting. If you had told me at the beginning of the year, that the major change I was looking for would involve moving to the Isle of Wight, I would have questioned it. But when the time came I was completely ready, and I knew that it was the right thing. I was therefore able to take action. My Cloak of Courage had done the trick, and my Sword of Strong Will had seen me through. If you are in a 1 year expect the unexpected and be ready to take action.

P.S. Don't forget your Sandwiches!

YEAR 2:

THE PARTNER

Keywords: Patience · Co-operation · Detail

Underbalanced	**Right Action**	**Overbalanced**
careless		*timid*
indecisive		*over-sensitive*
tactless	GENTLE	*interfering*
weak-willed	TACTFUL	*disapproving*
rude	FLEXIBLE	*devious*
inconsiderate	AGREEABLE	*cool*
	CONSIDERATE	
	CO-OPERATIVE	
	UNDERSTANDING	

WAIT FOR DEVELOPMENTS

CHARACTER BRIEF
Sensitive soul in search of peace and harmony

Costume	Props
Suit of Agreeability	Cup of Consideration
Pinafore of Pleasantness	Packet of Patience (large)
Coat of Co-operation	Scales

■ **222222222(11)222222222** ■

YEAR 2:
PATIENCE IS A VIRTUE

The Right Action this year is quite different from that of last year. The self-interest, determination and initiative are no longer needed. Your purpose and steadfastness will still be underlying all that you do, but success and good results are obtained now through diplomacy. Time is part of the result. Time is very important, and things will seem slow.

The need for a tactful approach in all dealings and undertakings is vitally important, and the exercise of patience when delays seem to hold up results is the background for ultimate success.

Dr Juno Jordan
Your Right Action Number

DIARY ENTRY
APRIL, 2011 – ISLE OF WIGHT

I have been trying to get out of bed all morning. It's 11.51 and I must have tried ten times. To be fair I do actually get out of bed. I wander from the bedroom to the kitchen, from the kitchen to the lounge, and then I'm compelled to get back into bed.

I don't do this ... this isn't what I do.

When this has happened before, and thankfully the times have been few and far between, I push myself through the inertia and on into what's there. I'm a go-getter, a person who makes things happen. But today this is not possible, and I have decided to try and stop fighting the energy. It would make sense to say, well there isn't any energy, that's obviously the problem. But I don't think that's right. What is happening is an energy – it's just not very energetic.

Believe me, I have tried to shake this off. I have given myself a severe talking to, meditated, visualised, used NLP and reiki on myself, and thought about my ritualistic dose of caffeine. I'm addicted to the stuff, although not really sure you can get hooked on one cup a day, but it normally gets me out to visit whichever supplier of liquid energy I fancy. It's just not the same at home. What's more the sun is shining, and even that isn't managing to entice me out of my malaise. I don't have flu, not even a sniffle, no bad back, in fact nothing to keep me in bed.

I know one thing. If I could give into it I would find peace. I know this because I can do it for a very limited time, and it is blissful. That feeling of total oneness with one's self. Just me and my very thought-less self. But then the voices start. You need to go and do. Well I have been 'doing' things for a very long time; and quite frankly today, I'm done! Husbands, children, houses, jobs, parents, study, shopping, ironing, building.

'Yes so what' I hear you cry. That's what we've all got. Us crazy, easily messed up, eternally busy human beings.

I'm sure my current inertia will be viewed as one of many things: laziness, lack of willpower, stubbornness, post move 'why on earth did I move here' misgivings. And I guess that's what keeps propelling me out of the bed, just the thought of what people might think. I can hear them now with their helpful advice. 'It will pass', 'pull yourself together', 'go for a walk', 'have a cup of tea'.

Well thanks, but no thanks. I am just going to stay here for as long as it takes, because I know eventually my spirit will re-awaken, because it always does. That's the thing about spirit. It's very hard to crush.

This has happened after a year of new beginnings. A move to a completely unexpected place, at an unexpected time, at the end of a cycle of divorce, adjusting to single living, and growing a business. This took courage; and courage once the adrenalin has done its job, takes you to a different place. A place of recovery. This place of recovery had been put on hold due to the needs of another, and now I need to play a waiting game, and be patient. I have planted seeds here in this new life of mine, but I cannot hurry their growth. If I can do what I can, when I can, and then pull back and wait all will be well (I say this out loud to myself in front of a mirror three times a day, as I am in much need of reassurance). I look back at myself and nod sagely. It is the advice I would give to another human feeling the slowness of a 2 Personal Year, but sometimes it's hard to listen to your own advice.

This new life, in a new place may have been unexpected, but in spite of the fear which wells up within me every now and again, I know it is the right place. You just know when something is right and when I get out of my head and follow my instinct, life becomes more peaceful again.

Two things happened at the junction of my 1 Personal Year and 2 Personal Year which were to stop me in my tracks and put any recovery on hold. Actually the result felt like stasis, as one event pulled me forward and the other pulled me back. Whichever way you look at it I was stuck at a red light. The week that I was due to take possession of my new flat, I went on a course in Oxford run by an organisation called SAPERE. The Society for the Advancement of Philosophical Enquiry and Reflection in Education. The name of the Society filled me with renewed hope, along with the urge to take on board new ideas, and mix with people of the same mind. I dithered for a while before I booked it, as I was about to undertake a monumental change, but I was hungry for something which would guide me on my way to a new life on the Isle of Wight. And so, in the three days preceding my move, I made my way to Oxford, and opened my mind to a system of education which I could use alongside the programme I was developing. I felt a rush of excitement coursing through my body, the like of which I hadn't felt for a very long time, pulling me forward at a rate of knots.

The second thing at the junction, was a very sick person in need of help. I had known him since childhood. He had stolen the limelight as one of Fagin's boys, whilst I was attempting to shine as a villager, in the back row of the chorus in a production of *Oliver*.

He had a special talent, and always managed to shine no matter who else was on the stage. Our paths had crossed many times, and he was one of the most charismatic people I knew. He had gone on to achieve success in marketing and TV, and I had been out of touch for many years. But our paths had crossed again, when he directed a charity show in honour of a mutual friend.

We kept in touch during my move to the Isle of Wight, and when a trip he was about to make to India fell through, he was at a loose end. I asked him if he would like to take on the rental of the cottage I had been stuck with, having made a quick decision on the purchase of my flat. There were three months left on the contract. He jumped at the chance, leaving me with a feeling of relief regarding the financial commitment I had taken on.

I knew his fondness for a gin and tonic, but what I didn't realise was that he was an alcoholic. Something I appeared to be a little naive about. He didn't drive, and I had brought him back over from the mainland, on my way back between Christmas and New Year. I hadn't seen him for about a month preceding this, and as we sat on the ferry, I realised that his eyes were yellow, and his stomach swollen. The cottage was cold and a little damp, as I had been absent for a while due to the move, and I could see that he was just not well enough to be there on his own, and so we went straight to my newly purchased flat.

All I had was a blow up bed and a much loved leather settee (which I just couldn't get rid of in my 9 year), a bookshelf, lots of boxes of books, and various much loved random objects. Luckily, my sofa doubled as a bed which I was happy to use. The comfortable blow up bed, along with a very cosy electric blanket that I had been using, was given up to accommodate a being more in need than myself. My goddaughter and I had taken to the sales in Sloane Square before my return to the island, and I had ordered a bed, two amazing cushions (always a favourite purchase) and some small, easy to move units which would fit happily in my reduced space. However, they were not due to be delivered for another six weeks, and so we made do with what was there.

I was slightly thrown by the unexpected intrusion in my life, albeit invited, as I wanted to get on with making a difference, get my flat sorted, network, and generally get stuck into my new year. But the 2 energy which requires that you slow down, regard time as your friend, develop patience, diplomacy, and partnership, threw me on my back: literally.

Clearly I wasn't paying attention. I had done a lot of heavy lifting during the various moves, and my back gave up whilst trying to juggle several things at the same time, including a heavy rubbish bag.

By the time I had managed to administer myself back to some form of mobility, I could see that the state of my friend's health was very serious. My insistence on a visit to the local doctor was, it would appear, just in the nick of time. Hospitalisation followed for period of two weeks, after which time I did what I could to be a friend, and co-operate with the circumstances. I knew he was feeling better when he took me to task about my love of numerology. He had previously berated me many times, quite vociferously about the subject, ripped my developing programme to shreds, and generally poured scorn on my residency on the Isle of Wight. In the past this would have floored me completely, but I was sure of my path now, and instead of weakening my resolve, it was strengthened. I am grateful for this. People rarely tell you what they really think, but he did. No one could have been more negative, aggressive, challenging, and thought provoking. Luckily, I am a great fan of 'thought provoking' and we engaged in many heated discussions. Time passed slowly during the first cold and dreary two months of 2011, and as he started to improve and become more independent, I did my best to engage in the community, trying to make inroads into new life. But it was difficult, and I had to slow my usually frenetic pace right down. Nothing could be forced. There are always days, or months, when you just can't seem to get going, and this can be a blessing if you can give into the energy. Slowing down gives a completely different perspective on things. Take time when this happens and view things from all sides. If you have a 1 Life Path Number you may feel that you are best on your own, out front, leading, and generally that will be the case, but there will always be a time when co-operation and diplomacy are needed. There is something to be learned from all the numbers, and as you pass through each day, each month, each year learning to flow with the ever changing energies, you can, if you stay focused on what is right in front of you make progress. Awareness is key, and the slow pace of the 2 energy will help you on your way. Partnership and co-operation are always key in a 2 Personal Year whether this is in a business relationship, a personal relationship, or a relationship with your community.

As the life force came back to my friend, so did his reliance on alcohol. As his behaviour changed, I eventually threw diplomacy out of the window, and challenged him. The 2 energy is a wonderfully supportive energy, but can go way over the line and end up being used as a doormat. There is a balance to be found. You need to stay secure in the middle of the court to be effective when the energy kicks in, and be able to speak your truth in a loving way. His departure, post accusation of his return to drink, and my observations of his treatment of people having changed, caused his rapid departure, leaving me feeling bruised and unappreciated. I had put my life on hold, and gone out of my way to accommodate his needs. But I had stepped across the line, something I realised that I had done many times in the past, and the situation highlighted this feature of the 2 energy, which is strong in my chart. One of the most interesting things I realised about myself, and my ability to give during this time, was that my love and friendship appeared to be conditional. I needed to feel that I had made a difference, in order to keep my number 1 core value happy, but nothing was communicated back to me. It seemed that everything was taken for granted, which I'm sure it wasn't, but that's how it felt. This is a very tricky thing. Unconditional love would seem to be something only saints can manage, and I felt a long way off any form of mastery on this front. I am work in progress, and I am sure in my next 2 Personal Year I will be given every opportunity to practice unconditional love again. I know I can manage it sometimes, and I know when I achieve it there is peace to be found. If you can't give without wanting something back in return, than maybe don't give. Understand that whatever it is that you can give unconditionally, is enough. The change to conditional seems to occur when the line is breached.

My friend's departure leaves me weakened and feeling fragile. The slowness of the 2 year invades my being, and the circumstances of the first four months of the year have brought me to a place where I am unable to move forward. My eldest daughter very sensibly tells me to get back into bed and read. Good plan.

In the run up to buying my flat I had tracked down a local author. She had kindly invited me for coffee, and we chatted about the art of writing. You just have to sit down and do it she advised. Easier said than done I thought, I bet she doesn't have a missing 4 in her chart! Whatever her numerology, she had sat down and written several books, all with a local theme, and I was eager to read them. The first three books in the series had been sat waiting to be read during my rather chaotic start to the year attempting to play nursemaid. But now it was just me, and the inability to get myself going, so I give in and read. I can't put them down. The local nature of the books fascinate me along with the characters. Were they based on the locals? Had I already met them I wondered. The places all sounded familiar, and were located within a close radius of my flat. I allowed myself to go there, without once leaving the building. It was bliss. When I had finished I felt a little bereft. I wanted to be out there in the mix, but I wasn't quite ready.

The books had been a very easy read, but I wondered if I should be challenging myself more. I'd hate to think that I was wasting time. After all I am supposed to be building something new. I wander over to the bookcase and pick up a book on Einstein. Not my best plan. My brain is only firing on a few cylinders, and I soon realise that I don't have much chance of getting through this one. But I am struck by the idea of reflecting on my current time–space continuum.

Taken together, space, consisting of three dimensions (up–down, left–right, and forward–backward) and time are all part of what's called the space–time continuum. A non-spatial continuum in which events occur in apparently irreversible succession from the past through the present to the future.

All quite confusing.

But what a wonderfully expressed definition of something which is so slippery. Time can disappear through your fingers before you know it, leaving you wondering where it went. An hour gone in what feels like a minute, or time that seemingly just won't budge. That minute that takes an hour, when our bodies and minds hover in suspended animation just waiting. Children remain temporally unchallenged, until their world is invaded by the restrictive and challenging nature of time, pulling them out of their daydreams into a world, which is ruled by the passing of day into night. The sun comes up, the sun goes down, tides come in and out and yet we choose to cling to time gone past so much. We long for things in the past; we crave the possibility of things in the future, rarely content with the moment. My pen hits the paper as I continue to ponder and play around with the idea of time.

DIARY ENTRY
APRIL, 2011 – ISLE OF WIGHT

There is a bag in my cupboard full of someone else's stuff. It is sitting there quietly minding its own business, while the clock on the side table behind me ticks away, pulling me forward into the next minute, the next hour, the next day. The owner of the assorted 'stuff' contained within the bag escaped into his own space/time continuum, leaving me without a proper explanation in mine. The question, when I ask, 'what do you want me to do with your stuff?' is 'why is it in the way?'. The answer, after several hours thinking about this apparently simple question is no, not physically. It's right at the back of a cupboard which I have to stand on a ladder to access, and pushed behind an assorted combination of 'my stuff'. It moves along as time moves along. Problem is emotionally it's standing in the middle of my lounge, causing me to step over it, go around it, and at various times when reminded by external stimuli of past times, to kick it, unsuccessfully under the sofa. It just bloody well sits there whilst my emotions oscillate backwards, then forwards, backwards, then forwards, matching the ticking noise of the clock, which in spite of being digital is doing a very good impression of a grandfather clock, with a great loud unstoppable pendulum. If I could really go backwards into time, I might have said something different. Maybe in a different tone of voice, with a different look on my face, with a more loving feeling in my heart, and without wanting anything back in return. I might have thought more carefully before words had sprung from me. Half-baked words, unable to fully express my feelings, soggy in the middle, coming from a place of reaction instead of a well-cooked central core. I might have taken more time to consider exactly what it is that I am, in relation to another. But the words have been sucked into space, along with deleted emails, and disempowering beliefs, that I have visualised, put in a hot air balloon, and sent packing. I had wanted to make a difference, but I had gone way over the line in doing so, and clearly wanted something back in return. I seem to have a habit of collecting waifs and strays, and seemingly getting involved in responsibilities that just aren't mine. If I stay in the moment I can be wracked with pain, if I try and enter the past I am full of regret, if I propel myself forward I can replace the pain with possibilities; but the pendulum pulls me back. Living in the present, nice concept...

Difficult to execute.

Anyway there are plans to be made, and goals to reach. How can you do that just staying in the present? It can feel peaceful stopping in the middle, but it can also feel like denial. A shutting out of possibilities, a ditching of important passages of time. When you step outside of the 'now' space you can feel fear doubled. If I stay inside the space I am able to experience 'dolce far niente' (sweet idleness), time can do its thing, and I will remain in the moment. But is it living? Am I in denial of who I am, what I want?

Sometimes you have to take risks. Scary, adrenalin fuelled risks. Speaking your truth is always a risk, and I said what I had to say. Surely, this is the art of living. I'm nowhere near the centre if I can't speak my truth, and with this knowledge tucked safely in my pocket, I move on.

I was very fortunate, in so much as I had managed to buy my flat outright, leaving myself enough capital to continue my existence without working for some time. But it didn't sit right with me, even though I was spending my time networking, whilst chatting and drinking coffee in my favourite coffee shop of the moment. The more contacts I made, the more numerology bookings I undertook, the more I learnt through readings, the more I understood. But for some reason it didn't feel like 'proper' work. I enjoyed it too much. I needed to do something to earn some money whilst waiting for my 'right livelihood' to kick in.

Or maybe it already had. Somehow the Protestant work ethic finds drinking coffee and chatting about numerology frivolous. So I go with the guilt and answer an advert in the village shop. An elderly couple are looking for a cleaner for five hours a week. Sounds perfect, it would at least pay for the coffee. I like cleaning; it feels as if I am making a difference, and given that Rome wasn't built in a day, I may as well keep the building site clean. They are an elderly couple and it not only makes a difference to them, but it gets me out, I get some exercise, and I get paid. Win win. The gentleman of the house is fascinating. He is the brother of David Pears, a renowned British Philosopher and my interest in my new job is peaked, given my newfound interest in all things Philosophical. He is a mine of information and I could sit and talk with him for hours; unfortunately, the dusting keeps interfering, but I savour every moment I can with this wonderfully interesting and interested human being. I didn't see that coming, and felt truly blessed. I feel at my most alive when I am able to toss around ideas and have intelligent argument thrown back at me. It seems to press all my buttons, all at the same time, and I become lost in the search for truth.

Whatever Personal Year you are in, you stand in the centre of your existence. Sometimes your expression is pulled inwards, sometimes it is sent outwards into the world. Generally the even numbers are about our outer relationships, and the odd numbers relationship to self. The 3 Personal Year, 5 Personal Year, and 7 Personal Year give us ample opportunity to delve into ourselves, whilst the 2 Personal Year majors on our relationship to others. We live in a world where self is paramount. The whole 'selfie' and social media culture is very look at me, here I am, this is what I am, this is what I am doing, my life looks like this. But it is often a falsehood. Photos lie, and quite often so do words. These can all be taken at face value without further thought or exploration. Snapshots of happy smiling families are just that, snapshots. There may lay underneath a Pandoras box, or storage jar of difficulties, unexpressed emotions, tensions, and desires. I look at photos I have posted and wonder why. I guess they form a nice historical date line for my grandchildren to look at, but the received wisdom around the matter, is that we want to portray ourselves as doing well, looking great, and hailing our children and grandchildren, as the brightest and the best. I hold my hand up; guilty as charged. But if we fall into the trap of looking at other people's lives, and log on every half an hour to see what their life is looking like, we stand a good chance of losing our centre very quickly. Social media is indeed a wonderful distraction when trying to write, and I have used it many times. On the positive side, the world has opened up, providing more opportunity for learning, creativity, and connection. It also means that it is easy for me to stay in my cave, and pretend that I am in the real world. But in spite of my mostly overwhelming desire to retreat inward (saves dealing with all the messiness of life), I have realised I am nothing without a full cast. There is no room for sharing, no room for relating, no room for developing, no way of finding and refining my wisdom.

Wisdom is found when you leave the safety of the cave and dance around and wrestle with the questions of self, partnership, expression, process, freedom, duty, responsibility, spirituality, money, and compassion, and this is not easy to do 'on-line'. The 9 year epicycle gives you a wonderful opportunity to take each piece of the puzzle, put it on the table and explore all its possibilities. We are here to accumulate new experiences and knowledge, and the rewards would appear to be greatest when we engage with our fellow man.

And so, I find myself in my 2 year, with my audience in front of me, and a chorus behind me. The self-centred action of the

1 Personal Year replaced by a need to co-operate, to listen and be receptive to the ideas and thoughts of other people; to work in partnership. I start to forge alliances through network groups, committees, chance meetings, through work undertaken, and a genuine desire to be part of a new community. This just seems to happen naturally within the energy of the year, without my forcing anything. Looking back at my diary I am astounded at all the connections made and positive partnerships formed within the second half of the year. Whatever your new start in a 1 Personal Year, remember to take pleasure in the gentle energy of the 2 Personal Year. You may have planted a seed in your new Epicycle, but this will need time to germinate. It may be a busy year, but as long as you have your Cup of Consideration and Packet of Patience by your side, you may well find the year full of harmony.

It is fortuitous that I have arrived at my new flat on the island in a 2 Personal Year, as the start of my ownership is fraught with difficulty, and I am faced with yet another leasehold predicament. It's complicated, and as always injustice sits at the centre. But I face the dilemma with diplomacy, steadfastness, determination, and a much more confident approach than my previous debacle at Burleigh Wood House. This approach results in justice for all, with much less stress involved, and I am happy to have played my part. I try to wear my Pinafore of Pleasantness in all my dealings, despite the fact that I prefer jeans, and I make some extremely good friends in the process. It is wonderful to feel supported, as I stand in the glare of the spotlight, strutting my stuff and fighting for what I believe to be right for all. I speak my truth, something which had become easier during the previous Epicycle, and I feel as if I am at last making some headway in the self-mastery department.

My experiences throughout the year continue to be many and varied. I work, socialise, and journey to discover the delights of an island full of surprises. The word Architect drifts into my eyeline during a visit to Quarr Abbey, a beautiful and peaceful retreat on the north coast of the island. The Grade I listed monastic buildings and church, completed in 1912, are considered some of the most important 20th-century religious structures in the United Kingdom; Sir Nikolaus Pevsner described the Abbey as 'among the most daring and successful church buildings of the early 20th century in England'.

Daring and successful, I like those words, they inspire me. I visit the Isle of Man to see some schools engaged in Philosophy for Children, and I can clearly see what a difference it makes to their learning. I am greatly encouraged by a retired university lecturer back on the Isle of Wight, who agrees to look at the programme so far. I listen carefully to what she has to say, and find myself very much enjoying the input of another, which rather surprises me. I am pointed in the direction of Brian Mayne, Architect of a Goal Mapping System. I have been alerted to his programme via my ex-sister-in-law, who had experienced one of his seminars. She had seen a picture of him on Ventnor Beach whilst surfing the net, and suggested I get in touch with him. It was a very strange meeting, with many synchronicities. Unbeknown to me, he lived just five doors away, and was well acquainted with my ex-FASBAT partner who used to live in Shanklin. Later in the year I take part in his Practitioner Programme, and start to include his system of goal mapping in my workshops. We had travelled the same path via the Anthony Robbins fire-walk programme, and it was wonderful to spend time with a likeminded individual also bent on making a difference.

In spite of what would turn out to be a busy year I do, at times, feel very lonely. The number 2 is linked with the Sun sign of Libra, which amongst other things is concerned with partnership and companionship. I believe that sharing yourself with another human being, can be one of the most rewarding experiences we have in life. I hadn't ever managed to have a relationship playing the part of the real me, and so I hadn't experienced it at its highest level; that was yet to come. But I was finding out more about myself every day. Whilst waiting I spend time clarifying what it is I think I need from another human being, and becoming clear on what it is I can offer. Clarity in these matters is everything. I identify the times when I had not been honest about my feelings. I look at the parts I had played, and the costumes I had donned. I visualise myself standing naked centre stage re-clothing myself in my truth. I contemplate the word compromise, a word I have rejected. I have heard so many times that in order to have a successful relationship, this is what you have to do. But when I have compromised myself, I have always fallen down a large hole.

The word co-operation sits much better with me and is a key word in a 2 Personal Year. If I can make the choice to co-operate with circumstances, in a way which does not take me over the line then all is well. Words and their meanings get stuck in our heads, and can become a trap. When I hear the word compromise I feel that I am already on the back foot, and unbalanced. But when I replace it with co-operation, balance is restored. The number 2 energy can help you to find your line, sometimes by taking you way over it, and landing you exactly where you don't want to be.

People who have the number 2 as a Life Path Number would appear to be very loving human beings, who always try to put other people first. They are not centred in self, like the Number 1, but centred in relationship and partnership. When this is kept in check and balanced, the energy warms the world with love. However the negative aspect can be the desire to help too much.

This can cause them to trip over the line, fall flat on their face and be used as a doormat.

I spend a great deal of time pondering, this imaginary line, and how I can co-operate better in my 2 year without breaching it. Earlier in the year I had overstepped the mark, but the lesson had been reinforced, and I was in a better position to view the line from a different angle. As the year moves along, I really start to enjoy the energy, which although busy, is so much slower than the previous year. I have time to think, read and explore, becoming more receptive to the ideas and thoughts of others that step onto my path.

There is a hard and fast rule in the theatre; ALWAYS put your props back on the prop table as you will need them for the next performance. DO NOT pick up anyone else's props, and make sure your prop is in GOOD ORDER, and working effectively, even if the props person has checked it twice. Every choice I had ever made had brought me to the place where I found myself at the end of my 2 Personal Year in my 6th Epicycle. I had no idea what the next 7 years would bring but I was excited to see what came to me. Excited about the dreams I would dream, the people I would meet along the way, and the difference I would make.

With my props back on the table, and my costumes washed and ironed and hanging in the wardrobe, I can rest for a moment and marvel at my journey. My Independent Spirit is alive and well and in good order, ready for a new adventure. Bring it on.

EPILOGUE:

NOT EVERYTHING

FINISHES AT THE END

The journey undertaken from 2003 until 2011 felt at the time, as if it was wending its way towards a place of conclusion; a place where you can rest on your laurels. I had dreamt up new possibilities in my 3 year, moved around some building blocks in my 4 year, engaged in an exploration of self and place in a 5 year, formed closer ties with family and taken on duty and responsibility for myself in a 6 year, retreated and reflected in a 7 year, lost money in an 8 year through wrong action, leading me to take the correct action in a 9 year, resulting in a major change in a 1 year. But there is no conclusion, only better understanding and new tools to help me on my way.

Once you dream something up from the depths of yourself, something is set in motion. There will of course be ups and downs, corners and cul de sacs, because there are lessons to be learnt at every turn. Writing your script takes time, learning it takes even longer. Time is the essential element. Nothing can be rushed. Patience, alternated with appropriate Right Action, will help to ensure peaceful living once the vision is in place. The required outcome is the thing to carry with you. Make it the title of your play. Don't be afraid to re-write, add scenes, cut bits out, play around with the props. Invite new characters in as you discover what you truly want. The lessons contained within the numbers is a simple one, and even if they are something dreamt up in an esoteric dream, they can enhance your life and the lives of all around you.

1. Begin
2. Co-operate
3. Create
4. Build
5. Explore
6. Love
7. Reflect
8. Manifest
9. End

REPEAT

YOUR PERSONAL YEAR CALCULATION

EXAMPLE

Add the Universal Year Number, i.e. add up the numbers in the current year and reduce to a single number, unless it is an 11, 22 or 33. These are Master Numbers and should not be reduced, as they contain a higher vibration and more potential for growth. In the character sheets at the beginning of each chapter you will see them within the number 2 (11), 4 (22), and 6 (33).

$$2019 = 12/3; \ 2020:4; \ 2021:5; \ 2022:6$$

Then add the day you were born, and the month you were born.

Lizzie Flynn born 1st June

Universal Year (2019)/12/3	3
Birth Day	1
Birth Month	6
	10

This indicates a 1 Personal Year

The year runs from 1st January though to 31st December

Your Name	....
Universal Year ( )	....
Birth Day	....
Birth Month	....
Personal Year	....

YOUR DESTINY NUMBER

CALCULATION

(Your Life Path Number)

Your Life Path Number is derived by finding the sum of the Month, Day, and Year of Birth and reducing that sum to a single digit, or Master Number. The Master Numbers are 11, 22, 33 and should not be reduced.

Turn the number into single digits and then add together. i.e.

Date of Birth: 28/11/2019

Day of Birth (28) $2 + 8 =$	$10 (1 + 0) = 1$
Month of Birth (November) $=$	$11 (1 + 1) = 2$
Year of Birth (2019) $2 + 0 + 1 + 9 =$	$12 (1 + 2) = 3$
Destiny Number	**6**

Date of Birth : 1/6/1953

Day of Birth (1) $=$	1
Month of Birth (June) $=$	6
Year of Birth (1953) $1 + 9 + 5 + 3 =$	$18 (1 + 8) = 9$
Destiny Number	$16 = 1 + 6 = 7$

BIBLIOGRAPHY

Balliott, L. Dow	*Complete Writings V2, V6 Kessinger Legacy reprints*
Campbell, Florence	*Your Days are Numbered*
Chopra, Dr Deepak	*SynchroDestiny*
Decoz, Hans	*Numerology*
Drayer, Ruth A.	*The Power of Numbers*
Gilbran, Kahlil	*The Prophet*
Goodwin, Matthew Oliver	*Numerology – The Complete Guide Volume 1/2*
Guthrie, Kenneth Sylvan	*The Pythagorean Sourcebook and Library*
Jordan, Dr Juno	*The Romance of your Name Your Right Action Number*
Lagerquist, Kay and Lenard, Lisa	*Idiot's Guide to Numerology*
Moody, Harry R. and Carroll, David	*The Five Stages of the Soul*
Moorey, Teresa	*The Numerology Bible*
Ruiz, Miguel	*The Four Agreements*

ACKNOWLEDGEMENTS

My grateful thanks go to everyone who has ever listened to me talking about my interest in numerology, especially the sceptics. To Julia and Maggie for reading the initial drafts and to Garry and Debbie, without whose help and steadfastness I would not have made it to the final hurdle.

To the friends and family who have offered up their homes so that I could write in a different space, for feeding me and listening to me as I have tried to explain my ideas whilst honing my knowledge, especially Jen, Maggie, Tony, Jacqui, David and Annette.

To anyone who has offered up their date of birth when asked the question "so when is your birthday", and for giving me the pleasure of observing the look of astonishment on their faces when offering up some nugget about their Right Action for the year.

Thank you also to Rees and Ailie for allowing me to workshop my programme in their businesses and to Kelly from Lola Rose Photography for her contribution to the back cover. And finally to Bob, you are my rock and roll. Thank you all.